EMPTY YOUR BACKPACK

Unpack Your Beliefs, Take Consistent Action, and Create a Life of Meaning

SAM DEMMA

ADVANCE PRAISE

"Sam is undoubtedly the best person to speak about how to build a winning mindset and maximize life's opportunities. This book does a great job of balancing theory with practical tips that any student can implement right away."
– Swish Goswami, Startup Canada's Young Entrepreneur of the Year

"Sam has courageously followed his curiosity and through this book distills impactful learnings about life and pursuing paths less travelled. I know it will be a valuable resource to millions of young people, but I am most excited to share it with my own kids."
– Diana Kander, New York Times Best-selling Author

"Sam is a true servant leader dedicated to helping others. His book inspires action and is a must-read for young athletes, artists, and entrepreneurs."
– JeVon McCormick, President and CEO of Scribe Media

"Sam understands what it feels like to chase a massive dream. The insights and perspectives in this book will help you define your own "Olympic podium" and equip you with the beliefs and actions needed to reach your version of success."
– Sarah Wells, Canadian Olympic Athlete

"Sam is one of the most authentic people I have ever met and he is fearless in his pursuit of helping others uncover their authentic voices and living in ways that make sense to them."
– Ryan Porter, CEO of Ruutly

"Empty Your Backpack *is honestly the book that I needed when I was starting out my journey of activism. The book teaches people how to lead with love, be critical, strong, and successful in your path."*
– Hannah Alper, Activist and Author

"Sam delivers friendly and entertaining hard-hitting truths about what makes the difference between a life of pain versus prosperity. The sooner you know the concepts in his book, the sooner you will enjoy life on your terms."
– Kent Healy, Investor and Author

"There are so many pathway options for youth to consider that choosing 'the right one' must at times feel overwhelming. This timely book full of advice provides tools and encouragement for youth to follow their individual curiosities and personal dreams."
– Brent McDonald, Executive Superintendent of Education

"Sam's take on creating a life of unique purpose isn't only inspirational but actionable for readers who want to make a difference in their lives and in the lives of those around them. You can't help but be moved by his stories and motivated to find ways to make your own mark in the world."
– Codi Shewan, Keynote Speaker and Author

"Sam's book challenges us all to "empty the backpack" and be intentional with the beliefs, actions, and relationships that will accelerate us forward."
– Daniel Horgan, CEO of CoLabL

EMPTY YOUR BACKPACK

© 2022 by Sam Demma

FIRST EDITION
Designed by Mary Ann Smith
Edited by Rachel Small and Maya Berger

Paperback ISBN 978-1-7782725-0-9
Audiobook ISBN 978-1-7782725-2-3
EBook ISBN 978-1-7782725-1-6

Printed in Canada

This book is dedicated to you—the human being courageous enough to believe there's more to life.

CONTENTS

INTRODUCTION

What would your life look like if you achieved your dreams? How do you think the world would change if every person you met was living their dreams and creating a life of meaning? Call me an optimist, but I believe this reality can exist—and it begins with you. When you chase your dreams and create a meaningful life, others are inspired to do the same.

DEFINING THE IMPORTANT PHRASES

In a world that throws around the phrases *living your dreams* and *creating a life of meaning*, let's start by defining them.

First, in the context of this book, *living your dreams* means bringing to fruition *your* definition of success. Not what society, social media, or anybody else wants for you, but what you envision for yourself. This book will help you create that definition and equip you with beliefs and actions to help you move closer to your version of success.

When people hear "chase your dreams," they often visualize quick fame and endless fun. That isn't what this book is about. The process of bringing your dreams to life will be filled with fun moments, but it requires resiliency, hard work, long hours, and persistence. It won't always be fun, which is why your aim should be to find a dream that you believe is worth these challenging realities.

Second, when I refer to *creating a life of meaning*, I'm talking about living in a way that leaves *you* feeling satisfied with who you're becoming and the activities filling your days. This is a personal journey. In this book, I often link the idea of creating a life of meaning with making a positive contribution, but you'll decide what makes your life meaningful for yourself. A life of meaning is one that, when you're lying on your deathbed, you can reflect on with a smile, confident that you spent your time and energy on things that filled your soul.

MY MOTIVATION FOR WRITING THIS BOOK

I wrote this book because I want both those things for you. I want you to live your dreams by pursuing your definition of success and to find meaning by spending your time and energy on things that fill your soul.

When I was growing up, many of the people I shared my dreams with would interrupt and remind me that I needed a backup plan. They'd imply that there was no money in my dreams—that they were unrealistic and practically impossible. Maybe this sounds familiar to you.

Coaches would tell me the stats: "Only about 1.5 percent of athletes go on to become professionals." Counsellors suggested I study subjects I wasn't passionate about "just in case things didn't work out." And many friends supported me on the surface, but I could sense that their affirming words didn't align with their true opinions. As a result, I felt as if my dreams were just vague, unrealistic visions that would never become reality.

I was always confused about why people would ask me what I wanted to be when I grew up and then spend the next fifteen minutes telling me why it wasn't possible or realistic. Why'd they even ask in the first place?

Deep down, I knew my dreams were worth pursuing because thinking about them made me feel childlike and excited, but I was afraid I was taking the "wrong" path and often felt alone and isolated. When everyone around you is suggesting you do anything but the thing you want, it's easy to doubt yourself.

Can you relate?

"You need a backup plan."
"There's no money in that."
"It's unrealistic and practically impossible."
"Only a handful of people ever make it."

If you have a dream—a good, authentic desire in your heart—that people react to with one of the above responses, please keep reading because I wrote this book for you.

I'm young (twenty-two years old at the time of writing), and I've made many of my dreams a reality. I'm creating a life of meaning filled with fulfilling work, unforgettable experiences, and wonderful people. Many of the things I journaled about when I was a teenager are now a part of my everyday life, and I wrote this book for other young people who have dreams that others may deem unrealistic or impossible.

For many dreams, there are straightforward pathways with clear steps and educational requirements. If the pathway to your dream isn't straightforward, don't worry—you just haven't figured out the steps yet.

Hear me loud and clear: your dreams are not unrealistic or impossible!

I've been chasing dreams and making decisions that other people refer to as "unrealistic" my entire life. In the last few years alone, I moved abroad for six months, dropped out of university (more on this later), invested my life savings in a coach, presented on TEDx stages, flew around North America to speak in front of thousands of students, connected with amazing humans, and developed the confidence to stop caring about others' limiting thoughts and opinions.

You probably have questions. "Did I really just buy a book written by a dropout?" Yes, but this book isn't about school—it's about changing your beliefs, chasing your dreams, and creating a meaningful life. If post-secondary education is a necessary step along your journey, this book will help you embrace it, along with the other steps you'll be required to take.

ABOUT YOU

You're a dreamer who wants to make the most out of your life. You have goals and ideas that other people think are unrealistic. There are things you want to accomplish that might seem far out of reach. Even if you're not exactly sure what you want, you have a drive and desire to do something amazing with your life. If that sounds like you, read and reread this book. It's a tool to help you throughout your journey.

When you look around, perhaps it seems as if only a small percentage of people achieve their definition of success. Seeing this, you might feel as though your dreams will never come to fruition. Slowly, you begin buying into the things other people say. You end up caring about what they think and allowing their opinions to hold you back. Eventually, you silence that little voice in your heart and bury that childlike feeling because you think you'll disappoint your parents, your friends, and the people around you.

Let's flip the switch. How many times a day are you focused on other people? How much time do you spend judging others and thinking about how they'll fail? Do you worry about whether they'll disappoint you? I'll bet you don't have such thoughts often, if at all. So why would you think that others are that concerned about you and your dreams?

When you're focused on others' opinions, you're living a life that isn't yours. Now, I'm not saying you shouldn't listen to anyone on your journey. One of the most effective ways to "level up" and move closer to your dreams is to gain new perspectives, so learn from the experiences of other dreamers and people you respect and admire. But know that you don't have to take all the advice on board, especially when it starts with "When I was in high school . . ." Sometimes you just don't want advice from people two or three times your age. Much wisdom comes from experience, but the world is also changing rapidly. Sometimes people who've been out of school for only ten years won't understand the words you use, let alone the unique opportunities that exist for you.

One of the smartest things you can do is get perspectives from people who are living their dreams right now, regardless of their age. I wrote this book for that reason—to give you unique perspectives and ideas from someone who understands what it feels like to have their back against the wall, chasing a dream that no one else understands.

I don't know what's going on in your life. I don't know the circumstances or challenges that you deal with daily, and I won't act as if I do. The only thing worse than someone who doesn't understand what you're going through is someone who pretends to. I'm not your teacher. I'm not your parent. I'm not your coach or guidance counsellor. What I am is someone who can provide you with a new perspective and actionable ideas that can move you closer to your dreams.

BELIEFS AND ACTIONS

To live the life that *you* want to live, you need to focus on the two things you can control: your beliefs and your actions. That's why the first half of this book focuses on beliefs and the second on actions.

What you think is true (your beliefs) and what you do (your actions) are responsible for the results you've experienced up to now. The only way to move closer to your dreams is to have the right beliefs and take the right actions, and this book will help you do both.

My aim is that by the end of this book, you will feel your potential and carry a new confidence that propels you to action. I hope that you will no longer be afraid to live your truth and chase your dreams, even if it means temporarily disappointing the people around you.

I hope that you won't spend time trying to "fit in"—because instead, you'll be striving to stand out on your journey toward a meaningful life. I hope that you attract other dreamers who share your empowering beliefs and build some of the best friendships you've ever had. The fact that you're reading this book means we're about to be friends too.

My name is Sam, and I wrote this book for you.

PART ONE

BELIEFS

CHAPTER ONE

•

EMPTY YOUR BACKPACK

•

Belief: You Define You

It was an ordinary evening, and I wasn't prepared for what was about to unfold. After eating supper with my family, I returned to my office in the basement to prepare for an Instagram Live. That night, I was being interviewed by a young leader, and we'd be talking about leadership, the importance of service, and helpful ideas for young dreamers.

In the first forty minutes of the interview, there was great conversation and lots of laughs. Then we invited viewers to ask questions or share a little bit about themselves. One viewer jumped on and explained that they had two goals in life: to become an actor and to get fifty thousand followers on social media. I politely challenged the person to explain what gaining followers would help them accomplish.

What they shared blew me away.

"If I became an actor and had thousands of followers on social media, people at school would stop bullying me and calling me a loser."

This person explained that their life was filled with bullies, that they spent most of their time crying, and that they had considered ending their life on many occasions. Then they turned off their camera, and went silent.

The hairs on my arms stood up. I could feel their pain through my screen, and my eyes welled with tears. I found myself at a loss for words. This bright young individual had considered ending their life because of other people's hurtful words. Those words, repeated over and over, became personal beliefs. Beliefs that they carried with them.

The interviewer and I reassured this individual that everyone watching loved them and wanted to see them do well, and then we shared some resources that would allow them to find the help they needed that was beyond what we could provide.

After the call ended, I couldn't get this situation out of my mind. I felt compelled to reflect on my experiences dealing with words that other people used to define me. What I wish I could have helped that viewer believe in that moment is that **other people's words don't define your worth.**

Words are meaningless jumbles of letters until you—the person hearing them—give them power. Often, the negative things people say about you are a reflection of their own internal battles and have little or nothing to do with you. How would your life change if you truly believed that and allowed others' words to slip off your back like books in an open, upside-down backpack?

YOUR INVISIBLE BACKPACK

Each of us walk around with an invisible backpack strapped to our shoulders. In this bag, we carry our experiences, which inform our beliefs. We also carry the beliefs, expectations, and opinions that other people give to us—some good and some bad. These also inform our own beliefs.

Other people's words can hold real weight, if you let them. They can become bricks that you carry on your back, and they can occupy space in your mind. They can stop you from acting or they can propel you forward. Words can unify a divided nation or cause mass destruction.

Unfortunately, as humans, we tend to give more energy and attention to the negative things people say about us, rather than the positive things. This is the negativity bias. It explains why you can forget hundreds of compliments but not that one terrible thing someone said about you. Like most humans, you probably spend a disproportionate amount of time focused on the one negative comment, wondering what's wrong with you, rather than feeling grateful for all the positive ones.

After I speak at conferences and schools, attendees often fill out feedback forms to rate my performance. I'll never forget the feedback from an event I did in Alberta. It was all extremely positive, except for one comment: "Typical motivational speaker…"

The last thing I aim to be is "typical," so I took this comment to heart. It made me feel sad and frustrated. It wasn't extremely negative (and the event organizer still hired me to speak the following year), but I spent over an hour thinking about that comment and allowing it to bother me before I shifted my focus.

Maybe you can relate. Maybe you got a fantastic grade on a test but couldn't get over the one "stupid" mistake you made. Maybe you've allowed the negativity in your life to overshadow all the spectacular things that make you, you. Maybe you've been carrying around hurtful words in your invisible backpack and they're weighing you down.

Can you recall something negative someone said to you that had a lasting impact on your confidence and self-belief? If you're like me, you not only remember what the person said, but you can rebuild the entire situation in your mind. You remember the name of the person, where and when it happened, and, most importantly, how it made you feel. Left unaddressed, thoughtless comments from careless people can take root in your mind and, over time, become your limiting beliefs.

Imagine that—a belief that wasn't yours to begin with ends up being the thing holding you back and weighing you down.

Even a comment someone made to you when you were a child can inform the decisions you make for the rest of your life. You might believe "you're not good at music" because your parents told you that at the dinner table. You might believe you can't play basketball because your high school coach said, "You're too short." You might believe you can't build a new skill after university because someone told you it's too late and you should "stick to what you know." Over time, your backpack fills up, and if you don't stop to remove the beliefs that aren't yours, you may end up living a life that's not yours—and fall short of your true potential.

Shortly after my second knee surgery, my soccer coach "jokingly" yelled at me from the sideline, in front of the entire team, "Hey bud, are you going to get up off the bench and play or are you going to retire soon?" At that point in my athletic career, I was routinely breaking down in tears in front of family and friends. I'd limp around school on crutches with a bag of frozen peas strapped to my swollen knee. At home, I'd perform every exercise possible to speed up my recovery so I could get back on the field to play the game I loved. The mental and physical stress of rehab, doing an internship at a gym, and driving an hour and a half to attend practice only to sit on the bench and spectate was overwhelming, to say the least. Why on earth would the coach—the person I'm supposed to look up to and learn from—say something so needlessly hurtful?

It was comments like this, along with my own mental battles, that created my resentment toward the sport. My backpack became so heavy that after I decided to stop playing soccer, I unfollowed all my former teammates on social media and blocked the coach. Seeing or hearing anything about that part of my life stirred up deep sadness and anger. I hope that some of my teammates read this book and realize it had nothing to do with them and everything to do with my insecurities and internal battles. It took me over two years to find my peace and rebuild myself.

My grandma was the one who taught me that if you have nothing nice to say, you shouldn't say anything at all. Now I understand what she meant. Words cut like knives when they're aimed at insecurities, and you never know what someone is going through. Just because you can't see someone's backpack doesn't mean they're not carrying it.

It's obvious that my coach didn't understand the impact of his words, but the negative thoughts they created stuck with me for a long time. There are still nights when I wake up in a panic from a dream about playing professional soccer.

My coach's comment isn't the only one I've needed to remove from my backpack. Teachers who never taught me have approached me at school reunions to offer unsolicited lectures on why I should be in school because they want "what's best for me." Relatives at picnics have tried to convince my father to encourage me back into formal education, suggesting that I'm wasting my time and life. Luckily, I regularly take the time to empty my backpack, and my parents continue to witness the ten-to-twelve-hour days that I work in my basement studio and support me without hesitation.

Find peace knowing that people rarely see the full picture of your life. Let everyone share their thoughts, and nod vaguely if you don't feel like arguing, but don't internalize or hold on to the things that stop you from following your path. It's important to respect others, but you don't need to consume their beliefs and opinions.

You are your own best adviser. No person on this planet has gone through and experienced exactly what you have. Your experience matters. Don't buy into the limiting belief that experience comes from age; that's probably a message someone put in your backpack a long time ago. Sure, time gives you an advantage because it gives you the chance to try different things, but time can also be wasted. I know twenty-year-olds who have had more experiences than some adults in their forties or fifties. Experience comes from experience, so be confident in your decisions and stop discounting the power of your beliefs and choices.

WHOSE BELIEFS ARE YOU CARRYING?

Your backpack accumulates beliefs from many sources, including family, friends, school, media, religion, and, most importantly, past experiences. The latter includes others' past experiences. Often, close family and friends will project their beliefs onto you, so be careful which beliefs you place in your backpack.

Let's say your dream is to open a restaurant, and you have a cousin who failed attempting something similar. Ask them if you should open a restaurant and they'll tell you absolutely not—simply because their past experience involved failure. Find someone who runs a successful restaurant, and they'll likely tell you it's the best business in the world. In both cases, the other people are projecting their past experiences on you in the form of their positive or limiting beliefs.

Be aware that you may also come across successful people who will tell you not to pursue the thing they're doing. Carefully consider their opinions, as they may help you avoid a future disaster, but ultimately make your own choice. Even if they seem successful, they may not find the life they're living meaningful.

Remember, your definition of success is personal, and someone else's dissatisfaction with their work has nothing to do with you. In this example, however, you should give the successful restaurant owner's perspective and advice more attention than your cousin's (because the restaurant owner is currently doing what you want to do).

Filling your backpack with the thoughts of people who've never done what you want to do is pointless. A pilot would never ask a passenger how to fly the plane. When someone gives you unsolicited advice or tells you why you can't do something, ask yourself, "What past experience did this person have that resulted in this belief?"

And remember, people who are hurting often hurt others. Someone you know might be trying to tell you how to live your life because they're dissatisfied with their own. Sometimes, when a person can't do something themself, their ego wants to believe that you can't do it either. Don't listen to their words or place them in your backpack. Instead, find someone successful who is doing exactly what you want to do and ask for their advice. The rapper LaRussell said it best during our interview: "Impossible is the opinion of the incapable." [1]

START REPACKING

After taking other people's negative beliefs, comments, and opinions out of your backpack, it's time to fill it with things that will support you along your journey. The first things to repack are people who push you to grow personally and professionally.

As a soccer player, I was a midfielder. My main responsibility was to receive the ball from the defence and successfully pass it forward to the offensive players so we could score goals. My coach would always yell at me, "Sam! Check your shoulders!" He wanted to ensure I was aware of who was around me so I wouldn't receive the ball and then turn toward an opposing player. Similarly, it's important to constantly evaluate who's surrounding you in your life. The people you invest time in will rub off on you.

---

[1] Sam Demma, "Interview with LaRussell—Rapper, Entrepreneur and Founder of Good Compenny," February 18, 2022, YouTube video, 31:35, retrieved June 20, 2022, https://www.youtube.com/watch?v=6voMy7jySCs.

Whether you like it or not, you'll assume some of their habits and beliefs. This doesn't mean you need to cut off all your friends and become a lone wolf—just take note of how your friends' actions influence you.

You want friends who will keep it real with you while also being your biggest supporters. My best friend Lucas is one of those people for me. When I decided to drop out of university, he constantly reminded me to bet on myself. He believed in my abilities more than I believed in myself, and we would make time to meet up and talk about our dreams. I'm so grateful for our friendship. You don't need a large circle, but you need at least one person who will hold you accountable and believe in you.

Next, fill your backpack with the beliefs and opinions of people who've achieved greatness. Their beliefs are the blueprint for success. These can be individuals who inspire you even if you've never met them.

Weeks after I got my driver's licence, I started driving to and from soccer practice on my own. The drive was forty-five minutes each way, so every day I spent an extra hour and a half in the car. That quiet time alone inspired me to begin listening to podcasts. One of my favourites was The Sports Motivation Podcast, hosted by former professional football player Niyi Sobo. In each episode, he'd break down the mindset and habits you need to dominate your sport and reach high-level performance. I made a habit of arriving at practice fifteen to thirty minutes early so I could jot down notes from the podcast in a Dollar Store notebook.

I still have those notes, and eventually Niyi became a personal mentor. He's responsible for a large part of my belief system and early business success. On average, I consume two to three hours of music and interviews daily, and I encourage you to listen to and watch content that reinforces powerful thoughts and helps you dream bigger. Find role models you relate to and listen to their content on repeat.[2]

Emptying and refilling your backpack starts with awareness. Over the next few days, weeks, and months, try to catch yourself when a negative belief enters your mind. Write it down and spend some time figuring out where it came from. Once you can see that it's not yours, let it go. Remove it from your backpack. Set aside time to do this, again and again, until you reach your goals and find peace of mind. Life becomes more meaningful when you stop carrying around and acting on other people's thoughts and opinions.

The fact is, no one cares about your life as much as you do. And along your journey, people will say negative things. People might tell you that your dreams are stupid. They might call you ugly, or a loser. What you do with their words is up to you. Be selective about which ones go into your backpack. Their words do not and never will define your worth.

From this day forward, whenever you feel your backpack getting heavy, flip it upside down, allowing the unsupportive words and beliefs to quickly slide out and onto the pavement behind you. Emptying your backpack is a lifelong process.

----

[2] Russ, Eminem, Nipsey Hussle, Jay Shetty, and Gary Vaynerchuk are just a few of my many role models.

TAKEAWAYS

- Other people's words don't define your worth. The negative things people say about you are a reflection of their internal battles and have little to do with you.

- You have an invisible backpack strapped to your shoulders. Check it often to see what beliefs and ideas you're carrying along your journey. Take out the ones that are weighing you down.

- Other people's beliefs are often a projection of their past experiences. Not all opinions are equal.

- Repack your backpack with supportive friends, inspiring media, and the beliefs and opinions of people who are currently living your definition of success.

In the next chapter, we'll explore a belief that will help you navigate another reality that can be uncomfortable: your journey will look different from everyone else's.

CHAPTER TWO

•

ADJUST YOUR TIMELINE

•

Belief: There Is No Right Path or Time

My university experience ended shortly after it began. One month and fourteen days after, to be exact. From the moment I decided to enrol at the University of Toronto, deep down I knew it wasn't the right choice for me. That stage of my life was filled with self-discovery, and although I hadn't yet figured out what my passions were, it had become clear that I wasn't going to discover them in a classroom.

One evening, while my parents were out having dinner with my aunt and uncle, I sat at home staring at my reflection in my black laptop screen. I spent every moment in class thinking about speaking to youth and building a business. I completed my homework but didn't enjoy any of it. That evening, I had to submit a ten-page report about a chemical in mosquito repellent, and I hadn't even started. Instead, I broke down into tears. Then questions ran through my mind.

- Why did you decide to enrol in university if you knew it wasn't right for you?

- Are you happy with the path you're journeying down right now?

- Are you afraid you'll disappoint your parents if you leave?

- Don't you know that you'll be a failure if you drop out?

After two hours of contemplation, I mustered up the courage to compose the most difficult message I've ever written and hit *send*. There was no turning back. I crossed my fingers and prayed that my parents would understand. Here is the message they received while sitting at dinner:

I'm really struggling with school. I don't know what I want to do with my life. I can't find the motivation to do the work and balance everything and it's seriously affecting me. I'm not passionate about it, and I don't know what I'm passionate about. I want to drop out of school. I just feel like crap and I don't know what to do. I lied to myself about getting into this program based off of what I thought I liked doing but I was not being true to myself. Now it's too late to get a refund for the first semester and I really don't want to do it. But at the same time I don't know what I want to do and it's really bugging me. Can we please chat when you get home?

Moments later, my phone rang. My cheek, covered in tears, stuck to the glass screen of my phone while my parents calmed me down and promised me that we'd figure it out.

After dozens of conversations with my parents and my guidance counsellors, and listening to my own intuition, I dropped out of university. It was well past the deadline to revoke my application, so we lost $3,000.[3] Fortunately, my parents saw how my situation was affecting my mental health and supported the decision. To this day, my family is unmatched in their support and excitement for me. They've been there every step of the way.

After I dropped out, the only people who knew the truth were my family and a few close friends. I didn't want to explain my thought process. When people asked, "How's school going?" I'd shrug and say, "It's going really well!" Society had taught me that most people would treat me differently and write me off if they knew the decision I'd made. Today, I share my story proudly, but at that time I was carrying the belief that I should be embarrassed.

What I needed during that transitional time was someone to reassure me that everything was going to be okay. Someone to explain this truth: **Your path and timeline may not look like everyone else's, and that's okay. There is no right path or right time.**

I dropped out of school so I could drop into my dreams. Education is a lifelong process, and it's not confined to the walls of a school. Your education will continue as long as you remain open-minded and curious while pursuing knowledge. There was no course that would teach me how to become a youth speaker and creative entrepreneur—and even if there were, my best teachers and lessons would come in the form of other speakers and my personal experiences.

---

[3] All dollar amounts are in Canadian dollars unless otherwise specified.

One of the first things I did after deciding to pursue this path was Google "youth speaker" and call everyone on the first five results pages. I explained my ambitions and kindly asked a few questions about the business and the art of speaking to students.

Almost everyone had time for me. I took pages of notes from those phone calls and keep them in a binder labelled "Inspiring Calls."

YOU VERSUS SOCIAL PROOF

My decision to drop out of school was one of the toughest I've ever made—not because I doubted my abilities, but because I met so much internal resistance. Following your dreams is difficult when your intuition is nudging you to do the opposite of everyone around you, especially the people you love and care about the most. But this resistance to follow my heart made me curious.

Why is it that if you choose to pursue a different path than most people, you feel like an outcast? It's because of what psychologist Robert Cialdini[4] calls "social proof."[4] Social proof is the theory that we copy the people around us in an attempt to take part in what we think is correct behaviour. Right after high school, all my friends went to university and college. I was the only person in the group who chose to pursue an entrepreneurial path. I did the opposite of almost everyone my age, which made me feel as if I were making the wrong choice. Social proof was working against my decision.

Look at the outfit you're wearing right now; chances are, you purchased at least one item because you saw it on someone else. Or maybe you were

---

[4] Robert B. Cialdini, *Influence, The Psychology of Persuasion* (New York: Harper Business, 2021).

standing in line at Starbucks recently and everyone had their phones out, so you pulled out yours as well. These are small examples, but social proof also plays a role in your larger decisions. And the scary part is that you might not even realize it.

Society does a great job of painting a picture of the perfect life timeline. Start high school at thirteen, graduate high school at seventeen, enrol in post-secondary education at eighteen, graduate at twenty-two, get married at twenty-five, have two kids by thirty, and work a job until you're sixty. Then you can retire, and hopefully you've saved enough money to travel and enjoy your life, now that you have the free time. If you're not following this path, you naturally feel resistance, and social proof is to blame. It's the reason you might think taking a gap year or not pursuing post-secondary education is bad. It's the reason you feel behind if you decide to do things differently.

Think about this: Millions of high school students around the world have been conditioned to believe that the next "correct" step in life is to attend university or college. Your parents and teachers were likelyconditioned to believe the same. Please don't get me wrong—post-secondary education can be a fantastic option. It's just not the only option. Many successful and happy people have taken different paths.

While writing this book, I interviewed several students and educators about their life timelines. Sara Daddario, an educator from California, shared the following helpful analogy. If you were at home and your friend was throwing a party, how might you get there? You could walk, run, ride a bike, take an Uber, pay a friend to drive you, ask your parents to drive you, hitch a ride with the pizza delivery guy—the list goes on and on. Each of these options will get you to the same destination but at different times. You will arrive at the party no matter which option you choose; the method of transportation you take is what makes your life's timeline unique and exciting.[5]

What we're rarely told is that every path is valid. When I was considering dropping out of university, I wish someone had told me that it's okay to take the path less travelled—that, in fact, being on a path with fewer people is a clear sign that you're following your intuition and are on track to create a meaningful life.

Almost all my role models have trusted their intuition and gone against the grain. Think about the people you look up to; I bet they all veered off the generic timeline at some point. I bet social proof didn't stop them from pursuing their dreams. Don't allow it to stop you either.

Stay true to your values and your dreams, regardless of what other people are doing. There is no perfect timeline. And even if things don't work out exactly how you'd like them to, it's better to try and be disappointed than to wonder what could have been for the rest of your life.

THE BUFFET

You have a serious advantage—age. Right now is the best time to start exploring off the beaten path. You likely have fewer responsibilities and people depending on you now than you might in the future. If you have few bills to pay and no mouths to feed, you have the opportunity to take risks. Now is not

---

[5] "Sara Daddario—English Teacher and Director of Student Activities at Kennedy High School," interview by Sam Demma, December 22, 2021, in *High Performing Educator,* produced by Sam Demma, podcast, 29:37, accessed June 20, 2022, https://highperformingeducator.com/sara-daddario/.

the time to play it safe. Now is the time to do the things that people refer to as "unrealistic." Now is the time to get off the standard timeline, create your own, and try as many things as possible.

Think about your life like a buffet: you grab a plate and take a little bit of each food available. You might hate one thing and not eat it again. Other things, you'll love and grab more of. The only way to figure out what foods you like is to eat them. Similarly, the only way to figure out what you love doing is to try different things. These new activities may take you off the standard timeline, and that's okay. Get involved, volunteer, give back, and try new things.

At the age of thirteen, I moved to Italy on my own for six months to pursue my dream of becoming a professional soccer player. The only rule was that I had to FaceTime my mom every night before going to bed, so she could see her "little baby." Living in dorms with over twenty-five other athletes from different cultures was an unforgettable experience. It forced me to grow up overnight and made me grateful for all of the things my parents did for me. In Italy, I was responsible for my laundry, education, and overall health. School was virtual and at my own pace. There was no one holding me accountable, which made it difficult to stay focused.

All decisions have consequences and unexpected challenges. In Italy, I was robbed, developed a severe allergic reaction on my eyelids, and got injured quite a few times on the field. I also fell behind in my studies, and when I returned to Canada I had to take a few grade-nine courses in my grade-ten year to catch up. Was it worth it? Hell yeah! I'm still alive, and I now see the world from a more diverse perspective. Travel was an option at my buffet, and I took it. Explore and embrace the options that resonate with you, whether or not they take you off the standard timeline.

THIS IS YOUR LIFE

Even if you choose a unique path, you're not alone. You just need to find your people. I was the student who took a fifth year of high school and a gap year and then dropped out of post-secondary education. I turned down job opportunities that would guarantee me a great income and invested the money I didn't spend on tuition on flying around North America to learn from people in my field.

I went well off the timeline, and I'm doing okay—better than okay. I find meaning in the work I do and have the privilege of making an impact on people around the world. You might be thinking, "Well sure, but some people in your life are probably pretty upset with you."

Here's another reality check: When you make a decision that challenges someone else's beliefs, they'll be upset initially. They might think you don't know what you're doing or that you're making a mistake. This is normal—and something you can expect if you choose to take the path less travelled. You can only hope that as time passes and you start to excel, your family and friends become proud of your courage and begin to support you.

If they never do, it's important to remember that **this is your life.** Your actions might disappoint other people for minutes, hours, or years, but acting in a way that isn't aligned with your heart is something you may regret for a lifetime.

Shortly after I left school, my parents asked me, "So, when are you going back?" It wasn't until they noticed how serious I was about my aspirations that their concern transformed into support. Once they saw me taking substantial action toward my dreams and goals, they stopped worrying about whether I was following the standard timeline.

This may not be the case for you. People in your life may not be as supportive as my parents were—I'm blessed to have a family that prioritizes my mental health before their own expectations. If you don't have the support of your family, change their perception with results. It's true that actions speak louder than words, but results are louder than actions or words when people doubt you.

If you're currently faced with a tough decision about your future, please understand that there is support out there for you. Others have been where you are, and what you want is possible. There is no timeline on the quest to chase your dream and create a meaningful life. Make decisions that excite you and stop looking at the clock.

TAKEAWAYS

- Your path and timeline may not look like everyone else's, and that's okay.

- You will arrive at the party at some point. The method of transportation you choose is what makes your life unique and exciting.

- Embrace the options at your buffet and pursue the ones that interest you, whether or not they take you off the standard timeline society has created.

- This is your life. Your actions may disappoint others for a few minutes, hours, or years, but acting against your heart's desire is something you may regret for a lifetime.

One thing is for certain: along your journey down the path less travelled, people will tell you *no*. In the next chapter, we'll explore how to handle these situations and turn certain nos into yeses.

CHAPTER THREE

•

BE PERSISTENT

•

Belief: Rejection Is an Opportunity

I had sweaty palms and my legs were shaking. I was waiting in a booth at a local Starbucks. It was my first job interview, and I was nervous. In preparation, I'd spent hours sifting through online résumé and cover-letter templates, trying to pull together the perfect application. It's hard to show your experience when applying for your first job, so I included words such as *dedicated*, *hard-working*, *team player*, and all the cliché descriptions you find in templates. I was wearing a dark pair of jeans and my nicest pair of shoes, and my hair was slicked back with gel.

The interview lasted only five minutes. The manager thanked me for applying and then politely let me know that I'd receive an email if I got the position. For days afterward, I'd jump out of bed in the morning and check my inbox.

Sadly, the email never arrived. I was embarrassed, and I had friends who worked at Starbucks, which made the embarrassment worse. Getting turned down by the girls I crushed on was tough, but being rejected by this manager was a serious blow to my confidence. His lack of communication said to me, "No, you aren't good enough for this position."

What I didn't realize at the time is that when it comes to your dreams, *no* doesn't mean *never*. It doesn't mean you should stop. When someone tells you *no* in a context like this, it's a challenge to get creative—an opportunity to provide that person with value.

Please let me be very clear. When it comes to other people's boundaries, no means no and you should never cross that line.

But when it comes to chasing your dreams and creating a life of meaning, it's likely that hundreds of people will turn you down or reject your application—and 99 percent of the time, you can turn those rejections into celebrations and wins.

YOUR RELATIONSHIP WITH *NO*

Do you remember how you felt the last time you received a *no* about something you really wanted? Maybe you were rejected for a job or a starting position on a sports team, from joining a club, or while asking your family for lunch money. According to a study that Mimi Doe and Marsha Walch cite in their book *10 Principles for Spiritual Parenting*, "The average child hears the word no or don't over 148,000 times while growing up, compared with just a few thousand yes messages." [6]

Over time, you've associated that word with upsetting feelings and defeat. Every time someone yelled "No!" and then punished you for something, it reenforced the idea that you should never engage in that activity again. In many cases, this is a good thing. It protects you and teaches you right from wrong.

---

[6] Mimi Doe and Marsha Walch, *10 Principles for Spiritual Parenting: Nurturing Your Child's Soul* (New York: HarperPerennial, 1998).

As a child, I accidentally put my hands on the glass fireplace in our family room. I didn't realize that it had been turned on for eight hours and had just been turned off, and the pain was excruciating. My mom ran over to find me crying, and the first thing she yelled was "No!" She explained that the fireplace was hot and I should never place my hands on the glass again. Whenever I got close to the fireplace in the future, my mom would yell "No!" in an effort to keep me safe.

When we're young, the nos we hear usually come from a place of love. The problem is that we subconsciously learn that *no* means *never*.

In business, about 60 percent of customers say *no* four times before saying *yes*.[7] That means if you want to make the maximum number of sales, you have to follow up with every customer four times. The last time someone told you *no*, did you ask four more times? There's a high probability that you didn't. Don't worry, neither did I. At least, not in high school.

When I first started speaking to students, I'd set up my laptop in a local Star-bucks—yes, I was butthurt from their rejection, but their drinks and Wi-Fi are unmatched—and send emails to school boards and principals for four to five hours a day. One individual said *no* but expressed interest in booking a program in the future. Every three months or so, I'd send him a note. My first email to him was in 2019, and I sent him over forty emails before we finally began working together in 2021. Today he is, by far, my biggest client.

---

[7] Aja Frost, "60 Key Sales Statistics That'll Help You Sell Smarter in 2021," HubSpot (blog), published January 8, 2021, updated May 6, 2022, https://blog.hubspot.com/sales/sales-statistics.

NO SEAT AT THE TABLE? PULL UP YOUR OWN CHAIR

Making your dreams a reality requires you to believe that you deserve a seat at the table, even when there's nothing in your life to prove it. It requires you to shoot your shot and ask for the things you want with the certainty that you deserve them. Let's be real—it's difficult when people tell you *no* because it feels personal. Someone is turning you down or suggesting that you're not good enough.

But what if you chose to redefine the word *no*?

What if next time someone told you there was no seat for you at the table, you pulled up your own chair? Not only would you make an impression, but people would also likely respect your confidence and determination. Stop waiting for people to give you permission to act. If you want to achieve your goals, you can't let a two-letter word stop you.

It's worth stating again: this entire chapter refers to nos in the context of business interactions only.

Right now, decide that in the context of business, *no* doesn't mean *stop*. Instead, see it as a challenge to get more creative in your request. When you hear *no*, ask yourself, "How can I provide this person with value and ask again in a more creative way?"

On November 5, 2020, I sent an email to someone I greatly admired inviting him to appear on my podcast, *The High Performing Student*. An international expert on self-confidence, he's represented by the largest speakers' agency in the world, has delivered a TEDx talk that garnered more than 20 million views, and routinely appears in the news to discuss his work. His name was on a short list of people whom I planned to interview in 2021. The next morning, I received a response from his assistant explaining that his busy schedule wouldn't allow for participation in a podcast interview.

High school Sam would have stopped there. I would have assumed that this *no* meant *stop* and taken his name off my short list. I could have convinced myself that persisting would be disrespectful. Thankfully, this version of Sam didn't stop. Instead, I asked myself how I could provide value to this person and ask again in a more creative way.

First, I decided I'd try to figure out why he said *no*. There are only a handful of reasons someone will turn down a professional opportunity. Maybe he thought I wasn't qualified. Maybe he didn't think it would be worth his time. So, instead of simply thanking the assistant for their consideration, I asked a question:

Good morning! Thank you for your consideration :)

Would it be too much to ask what the qualifying criteria are to commit to a podcast interview? I totally understand that right now it may not be mutually beneficial as I have a medium-sized audience, but if you would kindly let me know the numbers that would make sense, I will set a new goal and reach out in the future.

Warmly, Sam

People recognize persistence and determination. When you ask again, in a respectful, creative manner, people will be impressed. If you're one of the few who doesn't stop the first time they hear *no*, you separate yourself from the crowd in a powerful way. Don't take my word for it, though.

Their email response explained that they admired the follow up, and provided the three criteria they consider when confirming a podcast booking. They closely consider podcast requests when the host has a large podcast audience, social media following, and some notable past guests.

Along with this thoughtful response, they emailed me a link to download one of the speaker's online resources—a workbook related to building self-confidence. This wasn't the email I was hoping for, but it provided me with even more creative options. If someone takes the time to release something into the world, such as a workbook, they're probably proud of it. I downloaded that resource and spent an hour reading it and reviewing the page on the speaker's website from which I'd downloaded it.

While reviewing the webpage, I noticed a few things that could be rewritten to make a bigger impact, so I sent another email humbly sharing a few suggestions. That email got an immediate grateful response. Now that I'd provided value and displayed my persistence, there was only one thing left to do—ask again in a more creative way.

This idea of providing value before making a request isn't a new one. Serial entrepreneur and social media maverick Gary Vaynerchuk released a book in 2013 titled *Jab, Jab, Jab, Right Hook*.[8] Its premise is that you should provide your fans, followers, clients, or anybody you plan to make a request from with value, value, value, before you make your ask.

---

[8] Gary Vaynerchuk, *Jab, Jab, Jab, Right Hook: How to Tell Your Story in a Noisy Social World* (New York: Harper Business, 2013).

I waited two months before sending another email. It included a short, personalized video that explained why I thought students needed to hear what the speaker had to share. In my video, I mentioned a webpage I built that we could use to promote the episode if he changed his mind and decided he wanted to come on the show. My hope was that he would be impressed with my persistence and have a change of heart.

When you stop asking for permission and act as if you deserve what you're asking for, people take you more seriously. Want to see what the webpage looked like? Send me an email at book@samdemma.com and I'll share the link with you.

Less than sixty minutes after I hit *send*, I received another email. This time, without a rejection. Instead, it outlined how impressed they were with the persistence, creativity, and ambition in the approach. They kindly requested dates for a podcast interview and mentioned their excitement to collaborate. As a result of my persistence and creativity, you can listen to episode #153 of *The High Performing Student* podcast with special guest Dr. Ivan Joseph.[9] His assistant had explained that podcast appearances were based on specific criteria: size of podcast audience, size of social media audience, and past guests. I didn't have outstanding results in any of those categories, and his *no* still transformed into a *yes*.

Your persistence has the power to change the criteria people use to make their decisions.

---

[9] "Dr. Ivan Joseph—TED talk (20M+ views), Speaker, Author and Self-Confidence Expert," interview by Sam Demma, February 9, 2021, in *High Performing Student*, produced by Sam Demma, podcast, accessed June 20, 2022, https://samdemma.com/dr-ivan-joseph-self-confidence-expert/

SHIFT YOUR FOCUS

Recently, one of my best friends didn't get a job he really wanted. Together, he and I wrote a letter (by hand) to the hiring managers who had interviewed him. The letter expressed his gratitude for the opportunity to interview and thanked them for the time they personally invested in his potential. Shortly thereafter, my friend secured a job at another company and stopped reaching out to hiring managers; but, if he had single-mindedly gone after the first job, his next step may have been sending a video email, showing up at the office in person, or mailing another letter. Regardless, the act of writing the letter increased the chances of these managers' giving him another chance, and it left the door open for follow-up activities if my friend chose to pursue the first job (or another job at that company) in the future.

Assuming the hiring managers had interviewed fifty applicants, do you think anyone else who was rejected took the time to hand-write a letter of gratitude? Probably not. **When you are willing to do the things no one else does, you increase the chances of getting the results that no one else will.**

The actions and beliefs of others, including hiring managers, are outside your control, and spending time on things you can't control will lead to frustration and sadness. Instead, focus on the two things you can control: your beliefs and your actions. Shift your focus to the beliefs you're carrying, and brainstorm actions you can take to change the outcome. Although you can't control the beliefs and actions of others, your choices can certainty influence them. If I'd sent a handwritten letter, or even followed up over email, after being rejected by Starbucks, maybe you wouldn't have read the story at the beginning of this chapter. Maybe their *no* would have transformed into a *yes.*

Right now, you can decide that in a business context, *no* is a challenge to be more creative and an opportunity to provide people with value. You can decide to stop asking or waiting for permission to act and take action, regardless of the eventual outcome.

When you start reframing *no* in this way, there is nothing you can't do and no person you can't meet. Nothing outside of you can stop you from achieving your goals and dreams. Sure, some goals will require more creativity, time, and effort, but if you're willing to put in the ten thousand hours (more on this idea in Chapter 7), anything is up for grabs. So, the next time someone tells you *no*, smile and get back to work.

TAKEAWAYS

- When someone tells you *no* in a business context, it's a challenge to get more creative and an opportunity to provide that person with value.

- Stop waiting for people to give you permission to act. Move with confidence and ask for what you believe you deserve.

- When you are willing to do the things no one else does, you're more likely to get the results that no one else will.

- Your persistence has the power to change the criteria people use to make their decisions.

- Shift your focus to the things you can control and brainstorm the actions you can take to change your outcomes.

When a hiring manager or a potential client or collaborator says *no*, it's not actually the word that stops you—it's **your belief** that stops you. What you choose to believe and what you define as possible lead to your outcomes. We'll go into this in more depth in the next chapter, where you'll read about the 120 bags of garbage stacked in my backyard.

CHAPTER FOUR

•

BUILD YOUR OWN TOWER OF TRASH

•

Belief: You Decide What's Possible

There were over 120 bags of garbage in my backyard. (Don't ask what my mom thought about that.) At the age of seventeen, my friend Dillon and I were on a mission to change the world. There was no time to waste, and if that meant using my backyard as a temporary dump, then you bet it was going to happen. Every few days I'd be back there, cleaning up after the racoons who'd rip open the bags thinking they contained food. For over three months, Dillon and I stacked the trash we collected and covered it with large blue tarps.

This was the start of PickWaste (so named because we grew up in Pickering and we were planning to pick up waste. Get it?), a volunteer initiative to clean up our city and encourage youth to use their gifts to make a difference. To recruit volunteers, Dillon and I would speak at local high schools, but when summer break came around we were forced to get creative. In the summer of 2018, I told my parents that we were going to somehow get the project featured on national news. We assumed that people would take us more seriously and that we'd be able to get more students involved if we'd been on the news.

Dillon and I knew nothing about writing press releases or pitching an idea to reporters and producers—we just believed it was possible. Maybe you're going through a transition in your life, learning a new skill or tackling a topic that you know nothing about. Know that the *how* will eventually figure itself out. What's important initially is believing that what you want is possible and already yours.

We had the belief; on to the *how*. An hour of brainstorming later, an idea bubbled to the surface. What if we kept all the trash we collected over a few months and stacked it in a busy public location? Being half Italian, I suggested we call the structure the Leaning Tower of Trash. The idea was born—but more importantly, both of us believed it was possible.

Ideas are everywhere. All success starts with an idea, and all art forms are the execution of ideas. Everything you see around you was once an idea in someone's head. **Ideas are powerful, but only when people are courageous enough to believe in their impact and execute them.**

SWEATY ARMPITS

The first inspirational speech I delivered was on October 7, 2017. The audience was 800 high school students from my school, and I had the daunting task of convincing them to go outside and pick up garbage. To say I was nervous is an understatement. I practised in front of a brick wall at least a hundred times. Still, the words didn't come out right on the big day. I paced back and forth, talked way too quickly, and made no eye contact. By the end of my speech, circles of sweat were visible underneath both of my armpits. Looking back at the video—yes, it was filmed—makes me cringe, and I almost convinced myself to never share it. Here's the thing, though: I believed I was good, even when I sucked. I kept trying, again and again. Belief in your abilities, when there's no proof of them in your current reality, points toward greatness. It's a prerequisite to any type of success.

The first time you do anything, you likely won't be great at it. But if you stay patient and consistent, you'll improve. Believe in yourself regardless of what anybody tells you. You must believe in what you want so much that you're willing to take whatever action is required. Self-belief is the first step in bringing any idea to life.

In his book *Secrets of the Millionaire Mind*, T. Harv Eker uses the acronym BEAR, which stands for *beliefs*, *emotions*, *actions*, and *results*, to explain that your beliefs lead to your emotions, your emotions lead to your actions, and your actions lead to your results. If you want to achieve different results, you must therefore first change what you're choosing to believe about yourself and your situation.[10]

It's safe to say that Dillon and I strongly believed we could get the news to cover our event. Shortly after committing to the idea, we made our first call. We hoped we could stack our trash tower outside the Pickering city hall building, thinking that if the city got behind our idea there was a greater chance

---

[10] T. Harv Eker, *Secrets of the Millionaire Mind: Mastering the Inner Game of Wealth* (Toronto: Collins, 2019).

that the news outlets would show. Unfortunately, the city quickly turned down the idea due to safety and liability issues.

Your ideas will meet resistance; when they do, your belief in their future impact is what will keep you going. Sometimes it takes eighty-seven executed ideas before people start believing in you—that's the number of songs that independent artist Russell Vitale released over ten years before his music started getting hot.[11] Sometimes it takes 217 rejections before people start buying into your ideas—that's the number of times Howard Schultz was rejected when he tried to secure capital to start his company, Starbucks.[12] Dillon and I weren't about to let one rejection stop our idea from coming to life.

PERSIST WITH PERSISTENCE

Since the city wasn't going to support our plan, it was time to get creative. Before hanging up with them, we asked if they would share their news contacts—the list of television producers and local news reporters they emailed when hosting city events. Thankfully, they shared that list, but they also explained that there was a chance no one would show up because they might have "more important news to cover."

Now we had a list of over thirty news contacts, but we still needed a location for the tower of garbage. Our next call was to our school board. It was summertime, so school properties weren't being used—maybe we could stack the trash in front of our old high school. It was adjacent to the main road and near lots of traffic, so it would attract attention. After going back and forth with

---

[11] Lyndsey Havens, "Rising Rapper Russ on His '10-Year, 11-Album, 87-Song Overnight Success,'" Billboard, December 15, 2016, https://www.billboard.com/music/rb-hip-hop/russ-success-interview-7624345/.

[12] Nick Wolny, "How Howard Schultz Turned an Entry-Level Sales Job into a Coffee Empire—and a Net Worth of $5.7 Billion," *Entrepreneur*, July 27, 2021, https://www.entrepreneur.com/article/378555.

the board for a few weeks, we secured a permit to use the front of our school for the event. As long as we cleaned up the garbage and everyone signed liability waivers, the school board was happy to rent us the space.

For every person who tells you *no*, there is someone who will tell you *yes*.

Once we nailed down the location, we needed to find a company to help dispose of the trash (by the day of our event, we had roughly 140 bags of garbage). We planned to borrow my dad's pickup truck to transport the trash to school, but we needed someone to remove and dispose of the garbage when the event ended.

I picked up the phone and called various local garbage services. After speaking to a dozen companies, I was given the contact information of someone from a local garbage service, and they agreed to send two garbage collectors with a dump truck to pick up the trash after the event. Never underestimate the power of a simple phone call. If you don't believe in your idea, you may never ask for help. If you never ask for help, you guarantee that you'll never get it.

Our Leaning Tower of Trash idea was gaining momentum. Once we had the location and garbage disposal taken care of, it was time to get local and national news stations on board. We found a template online to help us create a press release, a one-page document outlining the story and event information. A press release is what you send to news contacts when you're hoping to get press exposure.

Dillon and I spent the next week talking to people who worked in public relations. They provided great advice on the release and our overall approach to contacting news outlets. Once we felt confident in our press release, we emailed it to all the contacts we'd received from the city. Surely one of the thirty would love the idea and jump on board.

After hearing back from not even one of them, we felt a little discouraged. Maybe the city was right after all. Maybe the reporters had more important stories to tell. Our parents reminded us that they'd be proud of our efforts whether or not the news showed up, but Dillon and I still believed it was possible. We kept calling, created a second press release, and emailed twice as much the next week.

Research done in the 1930s revealed that a potential moviegoer had to see a movie poster at least seven times before they'd buy a ticket.[13] People need to be exposed to your ideas multiple times before they pay close attention. We live in an increasingly noisy world, and people today need to hear from you at least twice as much as they did in the 1930s. You need to be willing to put yourself in front of your decision-maker at least fourteen times, in a respectful and valuable way.

During that second week of outreach, things began working out. We confirmed our first media interview, with CBC Toronto. Dillon had built a great relationship with a powerhouse entrepreneur we'd met at a networking event over a year ago; impressed with our work, she'd given Dillon her business card and said to give her a call if we ever needed help. When we began to struggle, she was the first person Dillon thought to call. She's the reason that one week before our event, CBC came to my parents' backyard and did a

---

[13] James Kaatz, "Marketing Rule of 7's," Illumination Marketing (blog), November 8, 2021, https://www.marketingillumination.com/single-post/marketing-rule-of-7s.

segment on our work called "The Leaning Tower of Trash."[14]

Once we confirmed the first news interview, we used social proof to secure the rest. We sent out another email to all our news contacts, and the subject line read: "CBC is covering our event, why aren't you?" We thought it was pretty clever, and apparently it was, because it worked! Shortly after sending that email, we confirmed a segment with CTV News and a third one with CityNews.[15] Within the week, the mayor of our city also committed to speaking at the event. At this point, our belief was at an all-time high.

When you initially present a big idea, most people will think it's impossible; if you persist long enough, people will ask you how you did it.

BRINGING IT ALL TOGETHER

The event, Awareness Day, took place on August 18th, 2018, and was a huge success. Over 150 people from the community showed up, and it was featured all over national news. The mayor gave a short speech, and Miller Waste sent a garbage truck with two employees to remove the trash—all 140 bags—once the event was finished.

The event led to much of PickWaste's success, and the news clips are still online today, but Dillon and I had started working toward this goal with nothing but challenges and obstacles. No news contacts, no garbage

[14] CBC News, "How 2 Pickering Teens and Their 'Leaning Tower of Trash' Are Aiming to Clean Up the GTA," August 17, 2018, https://www.cbc.ca/news/canada/toronto/pick-waste-trash-recycling-gta-1.4788639.

[15] CTV News, "Two young environmentalists inspire change | CTV News," August 18, 2018, https://toronto.ctvnews.ca/video?clipId=1465685; CityNews, "GTA teen starts environmental movement," August 18, 2018, https://toronto.citynews.ca/video/2018/08/18/gta-teen-starts-environmental-movement/

disposal plan, no permits, and almost no support from our city. Dillon didn't even have the support of his neighbours!

Originally, we'd agreed to store half the trash at my house and the other half at Dillon's, but one evening Dillon's neighbour threatened to call the cops if he didn't remove the garbage from his backyard. I had to drive there at 10:00 p.m., wearing my pyjamas, to pick up the garbage and take it to my house. Luckily, my parents were in bed, so I didn't have to argue with them about the added bags and eyesore in our backyard.

Dillon and I had no public relations training, special skills, or knowledge. We had no idea what we were doing when we started. The one thing we had was our belief in the idea. Because we believed it was possible, we cultivated positive, empowering emotions. Those emotions led to relentless action, and our actions resulted in the success of the event. Our belief was the foundation of our success.

Your beliefs lead to all your outcomes. Your ideas will meet resistance, and it's your belief that will keep you going during those moments. Nobody can define what is possible for you unless you allow them. Sometimes you will have to try eighty-seven and 217 times before someone helps you bring your idea to life. It's your belief that will inspire you to persist.

Believe that what you want is possible and already yours. As Denzel Washington said in his 2015 speech to Dillard University, "True desire in the heart for anything good is God's proof to you, sent beforehand, . . . that it's yours already."[16]

---

[16] Dillard University, "Dillard University 2015 Commencement Address | Denzel Washington," December 10, 2020, YouTube video, 15:50, https://www.youtube.com/watch?v=ROiNPUwg9bQ.

So often we're told to be "realistic." Forget that. Be bold. Everything you see around you was created twice—first in someone's head and then physically. It's time you start believing in your ideas and defining what's possible.

TAKEAWAYS

- Success starts with self-belief. Ideas are powerful, but only when you're courageous enough to believe in your ability to execute them.

- If you want to achieve different results, change what you're choosing to believe about yourself and your circumstances.

- Put yourself out there with persistence. Most people think great ideas are crazy at first. If you persist long enough, people will ask you how you did it.

- Everything you see around you was created twice. It was first conceived mentally and then created physically.

A simple way to strengthen your beliefs is to dream. The more you talk about or think about your dream, the more realistic it begins to feel. The next chapter will help you gain clarity on your dream. If you don't already have a blank journal, now would be a perfect time to grab one!

CHAPTER FIVE

•

DREAM BIG

•

Belief: There Are No Limits

"The sky's the limit." I hate this expression. The sky is obviously not the limit because we can travel to space and land on the moon. I know it's a figure of speech, but it's time we change it. **The only limits that exist are the ones you place on yourself. Your limits are defined by how big you choose to dream.**

One of my mentors reminds me of this every time we talk about dreams and goals. He consistently challenges me to think bigger and aim higher. When I set the goal to write this book, he challenged me to start selling it before I finished writing it. When I broke down crying to him about how my speaking dreams had been crushed due to COVID-19, he invited me to a private studio with a stage, a tech team, and six television screens to show me how I could pivot and keep chasing my dreams. He's a visionary.

His dreams are huge, and being around him makes me dream bigger.

Quick terminology clarification: though I often use *goal* and *dream* inter-changeably, in the context of this book, goals are dreams written down with deadlines.

I was thirteen years old the first time I intentionally wrote down my dreams in a notebook. It was right before leaving to play soccer in Italy. I had terrible grammar, and the writing was almost illegible, but the act of writing down my dreams helped me clarify who I wanted to become. I started doing it every day, and the repetition cemented the dream in my mind until it became an obsession. Remember, the more you think or talk about your dreams, the more realistic they begin to feel.

Have you taken the time to write about your biggest dreams and goals? We spend so much time learning about subjects but so little time learning about ourselves. Both are equally important, yet we dedicate little to no time to the latter. If it weren't for my love of reading, I might never have started journaling, and it was a decision to buy used gym equipment that sparked my interest in purchasing the first book I ever read outside of English class.

DISCOVERING A NEW LOVE

It was raining the night my mom drove me into downtown Toronto to pick up dumbbells from a private gym that was closing down. Lee Davy was the owner—a built dude with a wizard-like beard. We spent thirty minutes talking while carrying the dumbbells down the stairs of his gym and loading them in the back of my pop's pickup truck. Lee explained that he was closing the gym to follow his dream of being a life coach and author. At the time, he was writ-ing his first book, *Conscious Endeavor*, and he talked about the books that led to his decision.

At the time, I hated books. If you'd told me in high school that I'd write a book one day, I would have laughed in your face. My worst grade was in English, and I held a belief in my backpack that I sucked at writing and reading. If I had to read a book for an assignment, I'd use SparkNotes to get the summary. But I left that Toronto gym with a promise to Lee— that I'd buy and read the book *Think and Grow Rich* by Napoleon Hill. While walking up and down flights of stairs, he summarized the book and explained that it teaches you the importance of thoughts and their impacts on your life. Knowing that I was battling knee injuries, Lee knew it would strike a chord.

Today, there are three copies of that book on my shelf. I've read it multiple times and I recommend it to everyone. I didn't even understand it all when I was a teen, but it kickstarted my lifelong love for learning. It taught me the importance of positive self-talk, writing down your dreams, creating mastermind groups, and many of the things you're now reading about. Since first reading *Think and Grow Rich*, I've spent countless hours devouring books, learning things, and building on my obsession with personal development. One of my "odd" life goals is to have a home library that looks like the Hogwarts Library in the Harry Potter series. Okay, maybe not that big, but I want a room solely for reading and storing books—a room with a fireplace, comfy chairs, and the kind of ladder that swings back and forth on the shelves. You know what I mean.

So much of my personal growth can be linked to books I've read and the lessons learned between the pages. Reading can be boring when it's forced but transformative when you're choosing books that you're actually interested in. So, keep reading. It helped me realize that life can be limitless. It showed me stories that broadened my thinking and strengthened my self-belief. Reading personal development books taught me the importance of setting goals and journaling.

Since my encounter with Lee, I've never stopped capturing my dreams in the pages of journals. Check out this entry from August 18th, 2020:

"So much on my mind . . . journaling, writing a book, creating a course, growing my speaking business, improving my health, learning golf, creating videos and so much more. Who would have known that you'd be here two years ago. What is even cooler is that you're responsible for it. You are where you are right now because you had a thought that morphed into an idea, which evolved into a collection of actions which all resulted in where you are today. This journal entry is a moment of reflection . . . wow!"

Every day I spend ten to twenty minutes journaling. Back in 2016, the entries included goals and events related to playing professional soccer, and while writing this (in 2022), the lined pages in my journal reflect my professional aspirations of building and growing a speaking business. You won't find any mention of soccer in my recent journals. It's a fact that your dreams will change. As you grow and life unfolds, you'll develop new passions, interests, and pathways. That's okay. Give yourself the permission to embrace every season life offers you, and keep pursuing your dreams as they become visible.

As you go through life, your dreams might start to become buried underneath thousands of questions and concerns about the future. Maybe they stop reaching the paper. Maybe you stop dreaming altogether. So many people settle for things they don't love. In his book *Understanding Your Potential*, Myles Munroe said, "The greatest tragedy in life is not death, but a life without purpose."[17] I think the greatest tragedy is a life without dreams and goals. Having purpose without the excitement of dreams is like having a colouring book without crayons.

YOUR BRAIN'S SUPERPOWER

When I was growing up, everyone would tell me to set goals, but rarely could someone explain why in a compelling way. It wasn't until I began searching for the answers myself that I became convinced it was worth the time and energy. I was even more surprised when I read about a little part of the brain that I'd never heard of before. Initially, it sounded too good to be true; but, as its magic unfolded in my life, I began referring to it as a superpower.

The reticular activating system (RAS) is a network of neurons located in the brain stem.[18] One of the functions of this network is to act as the filter between your conscious and unconscious thoughts—the thoughts you're aware of and the thousands of thoughts that happen without your awareness. Based on the goals you set, your RAS will continuously scan your environment for anything that may be able to help you, and if it finds something, you become aware of it by creating a conscious thought.

Have you ever played the yellow-car game? When you're on a long road trip, every time you see a yellow car, you say, "Yellow car" and punch the person sitting beside you. When you play this game, you'll start seeing yellow cars

---

[17] Myles Munroe, *Understanding Your Potential* (Shippensburg, PA: Destiny Image Publishers, 1992).

[18] Suzanne Stevens and Wayne A. Hening, "Chapter 2—Sleep and Wakefulness," in *Textbook of Clinical Neurology* (Third Edition), ed. Christopher G. Goetz, (Philadelphia, PA: W. B. Saunders, 2007), 21–23, https://www.sciencedirect.com/science/article/pii/B9781416036180100025.

everywhere! The yellow cars were always there, but your conscious mind didn't register them before. Your RAS helps you find more of what you're intentionally looking for. You give your brain a goal, and it will monitor your environment for anything that will help you move closer to that desired outcome. Pretty cool, eh?

Learning about RAS completely changed my perspective. Goal setting quickly shifted from a nagging task to an exciting aspect of my life. If you knew your brain would work non-stop to help you achieve the goals you fed it, wouldn't you want that advantage? Good news! It's accessible to you, and it starts with writing down your goals.

FOUR GOAL-SETTING GUIDELINES

Now that you understand why setting goals is important, here are a few guidelines to help you organize and optimize them.

BE SPECIFIC

In a four-hour program I deliver to grade-ten students, I dedicate one hour to dreaming and goal setting. By the end of the session, students have goals written down for five areas of their lives. After one of these sessions, I asked students to share their goals; among the statements that flooded the chat box were "I want to be happy," "I want to be healthy," and "I want to make lots of money." Getting excited about happiness, health, and financial stability is great, but all these goals lack one thing: specificity.

I jokingly asked the student who said they wanted to make lots of money to share their mailing address so I could send them a five-dollar bill. The class laughed, and the student said, "No, I want to make *lots* of money!"

"So, should I send you ten dollars?" I asked.

Catching on, the student said, "No, I want to make five thousand dollars this summer working in construction." The class went quiet as they realized the point I was making. Your goals need to be specific so you can measure your progress along the journey.

If your goals are vague, you'll never know if you achieve them. Focus on what would change in your life if your goals became your reality. Instead of saying, "I want to be healthy," you might say, "I will drink four litres of water daily." Instead of saying, "I want to make lots of money," you might say, "I will make five thousand dollars this summer." Focusing on what you want to change will help you create a specific and measurable goal.

Being specific is also important because different goals require different steps to attain them. Let's stick with the making-money goal. If I told you my goal was to make fifty dollars, you might tell me to cut grass, start a lemonade stand, shovel some snow, do chores, or get a part-time job. But what if I told you my goal was to make $1 million? Your brain would consider this in a totally different way and your ideas would change. You might suggest investing, creating a business, or buying real estate.

Every goal requires a different set of steps to bring it to life. Getting specific directs your brain to search for the information, people, and resources that will help you achieve your specific outcome. As I'm sitting in a Starbucks right now, the following analogy came to mind. If you told me you were tired and your goal was to get a coffee, you'd have an overwhelming number of options. But if you said you wanted an iced latte from Starbucks, you'd know exactly what steps to take to get that coffee.

There's a route to every goal—step-by-step actions—and the more specific you are, the quicker you'll be able to find that path and reach the goal. Don't worry if you can't find the path right away. Just be as specific as you can and enjoy the journey.

SET DEADLINES

"Yeah, man, that's a great idea. Let's do it by August 1st!"

Why did I think this was a great idea?

Lucas and I were on the phone talking about going skydiving. This was our third time discussing the topic, but we'd made no progress. When I blurted out "August 1st" without giving it any thought, I instantly felt a wave of pressure. When you add a deadline to your goals, they become tangible—and more likely to happen.

There's a theory known as Parkinson's Law, which states that your work will expand to fill however much time you allocate to its completion.[19] You've probably experienced this firsthand in school. When your teacher gives you an assignment, they also give you a deadline, such as, "You have three weeks to complete this essay." When would you finish that project and hand it in? In three weeks, right? What if that teacher assigned the same project but told you it was due in six months? You'd likely use the entire six months.

If there was no deadline at all, you might never hand in the project.

---

[19] Josh Kaufman, "What Is 'Parkinson's Law'?" Parkinson's Law—The Personal MBA, accessed March 25, 2022, https://personalmba.com/parkinsons-law/.

Deadlines work for school projects, and they also work when it comes to your dreams. Creating a deadline adds positive pressure and encourages you to take action—now!

As August 1st approached, Lucas and I scrambled to make plans. I was sweating when I picked up the phone to book a spot with a skydiving company. On the big day, we drove ninety minutes to what we thought was the head office building. Imagine how frightened we were when the GPS took us to a soccer field in the middle of nowhere. There were no buildings in sight, and the head office was an RV. Before signing the waiver of liability, we had to watch a video on a VCR. To say I was scared for my life is an understatement.

We proceeded anyway, and it was one of the best experiences of my life. You can find images of it on my Instagram page (@sam_demma). You'll notice that we didn't skydive until August 7. If that had been an assignment, we would have handed it in six days late and probably lost 20 to 40 percent on our final grade.

Adding deadlines to your goals isn't just about achieving them by a specific date. Sometimes you will and sometimes you won't, and that's okay. Deadlines are necessary because they add the positive pressure and stress you need to take action. So, the next time you write down a goal, make sure it has a due date. "Better late than never" isn't just a cliché, and deadlines will help you bring more of your ideas across the finish line.

READ AND REPEAT

When something is important to us, we spend time and energy on it, often daily. If you want to determine someone's priorities, just take a look at their calendar.

If your goals and dreams are important to you, spend time reviewing and *speaking* them to life every day. This could be as simple as writing them all down as a list and reading them when you wake up or before you go to sleep. Beside my desk, I have a list of my goals printed out and taped to the wall. I read them before I start working to remind myself of my priorities.

The act of rereading your goals instructs your subconscious mind to search for things in your environment that will help you achieve them. Make the list and place it somewhere you can read it daily.

TELL OTHER PEOPLE

A study Microsoft conducted found evidence supporting the "six degrees of separation theory," which states that every person is only approximately six social connections away from every other human being on the planet.[20]

With this in mind, it's important to get comfortable telling people our dreams and goals—because we never know who'll be able to help us, connect us to a person who can open a door, or introduce us to someone who can change everything for the better. Telling other people your goals will also help you build self-confidence. Think about it: It takes courage and vulnerability to share your goals. When you do, you give other people the opportunity to

---

[20] David Smith, "Proof! Just Six Degrees of Separation Between Us," *The Guardian*, August 3, 2008, https://www.theguardian.com/technology/2008/aug/03/internet.email.

build them up or shoot them down. Your willingness to claim what you truly want, knowing that people may judge you, helps you build confidence.

When speaking to a group of twenty to thirty students, I often try an experiment. I tell them that I have a goal to learn about real estate and would love to speak to someone who has worked in that industry. I then ask them to raise their hand if they personally know someone who works as a real-estate agent. Every time, about half of the students raise their hands. People know people. And when you become vulnerable enough to share your goals, you give other people the opportunity to become a part of your story by helping you directly or connecting you with someone they think can help you.

As well, the more you speak about something, the more real it begins to feel, and your belief in your ability to attain it will increase. That said, it's not necessary or appropriate to tell everyone you meet your goals. Sometimes, speaking about yourself can come across as egocentric. When you don't have a pre-existing relationship, people may not care to hear about what you want to accomplish. So, before sharing your goals, make sure you've built a good relationship or rapport with the person you're speaking to and have no expectations about the result. Build the awareness to take advantage of the situations when you should share your goals, and the confidence and self-belief to follow through.

YOUR INTERNAL COMPASS

Dreams don't just get you excited about your future—they keep you moving in the right direction. There's a scene in the movie *Alice in Wonderland* where Alice is walking through a forest in search of a dinner party. She approaches a fork in the road, and between the two roads sits the Cheshire Cat. Alice asks the Cheshire Cat which way she should go, to which the Cheshire Cat responds by asking Alice where she wants to go. After Alice explains that she isn't sure, the Cheshire Cat replies that, in that case, it doesn't matter what road she chooses. [21]

When you have dreams, you have the clarity you need to decide what road to take when you approach a fork. Dreaming allows you to make more calculated, strategic decisions. You can consistently ask yourself whether your current actions align with your future dreams; if they don't, you'll have the awareness to change something.

Imagine you're boarding a cruise ship and, as the captain shakes your hand to welcome you aboard, they explain that the ship will leave port and start a journey into the middle of the ocean in the hope of finding land before running out of gas. Would you want to get on that boat? *No*, right? Unless you love swimming. In reality, a destination is always selected before a ship sets sail so that the crew can lay out all the steps to a safe arrival. Without a final destination, the cruise becomes nothing more than a floating boat in the middle of the ocean.

To avoid floating through life, create a clear picture of the result you're working toward. Author Steven Covey describes this process as "beginning with the end in mind."[22] When you know where you're going, there's no obstacle or enticing opportunity that can stop or distract you. Cruise ships veer off track when there are massive storms, but because they have a destination in mind they can get back on track when the waters calm.

---

[21] Alice in Wonderland, directed by Tim Burton (2010; Walt Disney Pictures), Blu-ray Disc, 1080p HD.

[22] Stephen Covey, *The Seven Habits of Highly Effective People* (Provo, UT: Covey Leadership Center, 1996).

While it's vital to have a clear picture of the result, it's also important to remain flexible about the path that will get you there. Sometimes a storm can open your mind to an alternative route—one that may be more exciting and rewarding.

No matter how hard you try not to, you'll veer off track. You'll fail, lose your grip on good habits, and feel lost. Congratulations, that means you're human! Keep dreaming and focusing on your result during those times. One of the easiest ways to start dreaming again is to write out your ideal day.

YOUR IDEAL DAY

Think about what you want your life to look like once your dreams have come true. Here are some prompts to get you started:

Where do you live?
What do you do each day?
How are you helping others?
What time do you wake up and go to sleep?
What emotions are you experiencing?
Who are you with?
What possessions do you own?
What is your relationship status?

Grab a sheet of paper and create a blank twenty-four-hour schedule. Now fill in what you'd be doing for every hour of this day if all your dreams came true. Be as specific as you can. This document will become something you can keep by your bedside and look at every day—a simple reminder of what you're working toward.

A few things to keep in mind as you begin this exercise:

- If you stay on track, many of the things you write down today can and will become your life in future years. As mentioned, I've been writing down my dreams since I was thirteen. It's wild to look back and read dreams I wrote about years ago that I am now living. Doing so makes me feel an immense amount of gratitude and happiness.

- Your dreams don't have to be huge, but they need to be yours. It's true that you can't dream big enough, the sky is not the limit, and the only barrier is your imagination. But what you ask for you may receive, so make sure you're chasing a dream that excites you—something that truly makes you happy and isn't the product of other people's opinions.

- Achieving all your dreams isn't what's important. Not everything you write down will become reality, but the commitment and discipline required to chase a dream will provide the real reward: personal development. Worry less about checking things off your list and more about who you become in the process.

The goal of this exercise is to gain clarity on your destination so you can strive to begin living that life right now. If this feels overwhelming and you're unsure what to write, you're not alone. You may have never been asked to dream before, and it can be uncomfortable and confusing. Be patient with yourself and start small. Keep an open mind and whenever a strong desire arises, write it down.

THERE IS NO END

As important as dreams and goals are, know that you will never "arrive." Life is a continuous journey with no final destination. Don't fall victim to the idea that once you have certain possessions and have become "successful," you'll be happy. I don't want to be the one to disappoint you, but it's simply not true. Who you become in the process of pursuing your dream will always matter more than achieving a milestone.

Be aware, your dreams will change. As you grow, life will nudge you when it's time to pursue a different dream. What is not meant for you will not stay in your life, and this includes your dreams. As you, your passions and interests change, your dreams will too. What's important is that you keep pursuing something meaningful to you. Chasing big dreams gives you no choice but to level up and grow.

So, dream big. Bring back the imagination you had as a child, when you thought everything was possible. The sky is no longer the limit—in truth, it never was.

TAKEAWAYS

- The sky is *not* the limit. The only limits that exist are the limits that you place on yourself. Your limits are defined by how big you choose to dream.

- Your RAS is always working to bring your goals to life.

- When you set goals, be specific, set deadlines, read and reread them, and tell them to other people.

- Design your ideal day to paint a clear picture of what you'd like your life to feel like, so you can start moving toward it today. Let your dreams be your compass.

- There is no final destination, and your journey is what makes pursuing dreams worthwhile. Who you become while pursuing your dreams is more important than achieving milestones.

When you pursue your dreams, you'll meet people and have experiences that will help you make sense of the challenges and obstacles you'll face. Sometimes it takes years, but trust me, your journey will make sense in your future. In the next chapter, we explore the ideas of trust and faith.

CHAPTER SIX

•

CONNECT
THE DOTS

•

Belief: Trust Your Intuition

On December 28, 2019, I received an email from someone I admired in the speaking space. At that point, I'd been delivering presentations for two years and had dropped out of university to pursue this path. This individual was a very successful speaker, and when I started speaking I began writing their name in my journal and on sticky notes posted on my bedroom walls as someone I aspired to work with.

This person spoke at thousands of conferences and events, had TV shows and best-selling books and owned a very successful speaking agency. In the year before I received their email, I invested lots of money and time in their programs, and I even flew out of the country to attend one of their live events. My dream was to work with this individual, but aside from my discipline, dedication, and open mind, I had no reason to believe it would happen. Hence my excitement when I opened my laptop to find an official invitation to join their speaking agency.

Finally, here was proof that my dream of building a speaking business wasn't just a vague daydream. This email validated the endless hours spent in my Starbucks office. Reading it felt like a dream come true, and it meant that I could take down the sticky notes on my bedroom walls (my mom loved that). Shortly after receiving the email, I expressed my interest in joining their team and they sent me the official contract. I was one signature away from making this dream a reality.

The contract promised significant success over the duration of the agreement, along with speaking events, book deals, TV shows, and support from some of the best speakers in the world.

Sounds amazing, right?

The only issue was that I couldn't get myself to sign the paper. The duration and terms of the agreement didn't align with my values or vision, and joining just didn't feel right. The week that followed was filled with sleepless nights, frustration, and anxiety. On paper, this agency was a golden opportunity, but my intuition told me otherwise.

Being stuck in the middle of a tough decision sucks. In these situations, often the fear of making the wrong choice and losing something is all you can think about. "What if I miss out on a huge opportunity?" "What if I take on something not aligned with my dreams and end up unhappy?"

One of my good friends put the difficulty this way: it's hard to figure out the colour of a wall when your nose is touching it. Zooming out and getting a different perspective is important—but, let's be honest, it's a lot easier said than done. When you have no immediate proof that you're making the right choice aside from a feeling in your gut, it's easier to doubt yourself than it is to trust yourself.

I decided to zoom out, get my nose off the wall, and hear the perspectives of all the people I respected. I called my closest friends, mentors, and speaking colleagues, and 99 percent of them told me that I would be insane to say no. This opportunity was "once in a lifetime," and saying yes could "open so many doors that could take me years to open myself." Keep in mind, I'd dropped out of university to pursue this path and at this point had had little success on my own.

Even still, my gut was telling me this wasn't the right decision.

During his Stanford University commencement address, Steve Jobs said something that would be quoted repeatedly over the next decade: "You can't connect the dots looking forward—you can only connect them looking backwards. So you have to trust that the dots will somehow connect in your future."[23]

Jobs believed that you couldn't make sense of certain events in your life until they became pieces of your past. You just had to trust your intuition and decisions, and in hindsight you would come to understand why things unfolded as they did.

After all the calls and conversations, I was prepared to act against my gut and say yes. But God, Allah, The Universe—someone—wanted me to talk to one more person before making the decision.

---

[23] Stanford, "Steve Jobs' 2005 Stanford Commencement Address," March 7, 2008, YouTube video, 15:04, https://www.youtube.com/watch?v=UF8uR6Z6KLc.

RING, RING, RING

A few days before I either had to sign or rip up the contract, my phone rang. Someone named Tal Granite had found my website and called me. He explained that he'd recently arrived in Canada and had spent the last twenty years using the game of chess to teach leadership skills to young people. Impressed with my work, he had some questions for me. At the time, I was working at a restaurant to help fund my speaking dreams, so we agreed that he'd pay for dinner after one of my shifts and I'd answer all the questions he had.

A couple of days later, I was sitting across a table from this man I knew almost nothing about, and after fifteen minutes of conversation it was obvious that Tal could help me just as much as I planned to help him. He had an aura of wisdom that was magnetic. After I answered his questions, I asked for his opinion on my dilemma, and he shared a simple but powerful story.

"Sam, when I was a kid, everyone at school bullied me. I was a giant compared to my classmates, but despite my size I was always the student everyone picked on. Year after year I was afraid to speak up or defend myself, until one day, I'm not sure what happened, but enough was enough. I grabbed the bully by their shirt and firmly told them:

'This. Stops. Now.'

"You wouldn't believe it. That was the last time anyone at school made fun of me. I grew up hating those bullies, but looking back I think I needed them. If they hadn't pushed me down and called me names, I may have never developed a voice for myself. I may have never learned how to stand up for myself. Sam, what you're experiencing right now is a test from life. Everyone around you is telling you to sign the agreement so that you can find the courage to follow your intuition and develop your voice. This is a test to see how serious you are about the path you're currently on. You don't need any more advice. You already know what you need to do. Follow your heart, kid."

One word: goosebumps. Every time I think about that dinner, I'm reminded that the dots always connect—just not always in the way we expect. Tal helped me find the courage within myself to make the decision that aligned with the little voice in my head and the feelings in my solar plexus. He helped me look at the decision from a totally different perspective.

Trust your intuition when it's trying to tell you something, and have faith in your decisions. The picture might look confusing right now, but the dots will eventually connect. People might not understand why you're making a certain decision, but if it aligns with your heart and causes no harm to others, then their opinions are irrelevant. What decision have you been putting off even though, deep down, you know it's something that needs to happen? Make it now. Promise yourself that from now on you will always listen to that internal voice, even when it takes you down difficult paths.

DIFFICULT DECISIONS

A couple of days after that dinner, I called the owner of the speaking agency and politely declined the opportunity to join their team. It was one of the most difficult decisions of my life, and it definitely didn't help when the owner said something I'll never forget: "Sam, mark down this day, January 1, 2020, as the day you made the best or the worst decision of your life."

After they hung up, I remember turning off my iPhone screen and staring at my reflection as tears pooled in my eyes. Self-doubt flooded my body and my mind raced. "Did you just make the worst decision of your life?" I immediately laced up my running shoes and ran a few laps around my neighbourhood to let go of those destructive feelings, and once I got home I added a new event to my calendar:

January 1, 2020—BEST DECISION OF YOUR LIFE.

Nobody can tell you that your decisions are right or wrong when it comes to your dreams and goals. They're *your* dreams and goals. The actions you take following a decision are what determine success or failure. In that moment, the owner of the agency made me feel hopeless; but, as you read this, I can assure you it was the best decision I ever made.

If I'd joined the agency, I would have been locked into a long arrangement. The creative ideas I'd have generated during the agreement would have become the intellectual property of the agency. Large percentages of all my sales would also have gone to the agency. I'm intrinsically motivated and extremely willing to do the work, so this would have been the wrong decision for me—and waiting ten years to get myself out of the arrangement would have been soul crushing. Today, I love the path I'm on and wake up excited to continue journeying down it. As difficult as it may be, you have to trust that, at some point in your future, your dots will connect.

We're often encouraged to cross our legs, sit, and think everything through before taking action, and there was a time when all my decisions had to make perfect logical sense before I acted. Sure, reflection and contemplation are important, but people living meaningful lives also embrace the unknown. They spend time thinking but also chase goals that seem unrealistic. Logic isn't enough when it comes to chasing your dreams because all big dreams seem wildly unachievable.

Don't just ask, "Does it make sense?" Also ask, "Does it feel right?"

As difficult as it can be, I urge you to follow your intuition and have faith in your decisions. Thinking can only get you so far—sometimes you need to have faith and feel your way to a decision. That feeling, that little voice in your head and the pressure in your stomach that nudges you in a certain direction, is not something to ignore.

HEART THOUGHTS

Deep down, you probably have an "unrealistic thing" that you want to accomplish. You feel this desire in your heart but struggle to follow through because your head keeps talking you out of it. When someone tells you to "follow your heart," what they're really saying is follow your intuition.

Life is filled with situations where you need to follow your heart, and in June 2021 I encountered another one. It was my best year in business so far. I'd had over one hundred speaking engagements, interviewed over 120 people on my podcasts, and found myself checking off all my yearly goals. Life felt amazing and everything was going according to plan. But deep down, there was something I wanted to create that I knew most people wouldn't understand. I couldn't even get comfortable with the idea myself, so it was definitely going to confuse others.

I felt this overwhelming excitement and energy to create a spoken-word poem. Just so you understand, I'd never written poetry, played an instrument outside of elementary school band class, or even thought about making music before. It made no logical sense, but my heart was encouraging me to follow through. As I began seriously considering the idea, the other internal voice, the one that tries to stop us from acting, started spewing limiting thoughts.

- Who do you think you are?

- You can't just start writing poetry and music.

- People are going to think you're unrealistic.

- Stick to what you know and are good at.

- If you had been doing it your whole life, maybe it would be a good idea.

Dealing with others' opinions and emptying your backpack is one thing. But **it's often your perception of yourself, and your lack of faith in your intuition, that stops you from following through.** Your mind wants to protect you from danger and potential embarrassment, so it prefers to maintain the status quo rather than push boundaries.

The thought of this new project made me so uncomfortable that for a few weeks I told no one about it. I'd retreat to the basement to write song concepts and lyrics in my journal. The more I wrote and invested time in exploring this craft, the more comfortable it began to feel. The first person I shared this idea with was one of my best friends. He wholeheartedly supported me even though the voice recordings I shared were garbage. Remember, the first time you do anything you can't expect to be world class. At the beginning of any dream, the only important thing to measure is your attendance.

By the end of June, I had the entire poem written. I even got to sit in a studio and record it with a producer and audio engineer. I felt like Eminem! As expected, most people in my life were puzzled by my seemingly random passion. When I shared the idea with my speaking coach, he said, "Sam, if you'd been writing poems and music since you were twelve, I'd tell you to go for it."

I knew my coach meant no harm with his words and was only trying to protect me. In fact, he's so self-aware that five minutes later, he realized that what he'd said was coming from his limiting beliefs and apologized. He reassured me that anything that makes me extremely excited is worth pursuing, and he reminded me to trust my intuition and have faith in this decision.

That poem is called "Empty Backpack." The backpack idea that I detailed in Chapter 1 evolved from this spoken-word poem into a national movement. As a result, I will be travelling across Canada with a giant backpack to raise awareness about mental health and the power of beliefs. It helped me remind thousands of young people that other people's words don't define their worth. It changed the trajectory of my life—and, more importantly, it changed the lives of thousands of young people.

Over the years, I'd followed my intuition enough to know that pursuing this project was the right choice, regardless of my thoughts and those of others. But it was interesting to watch people battling their own limiting beliefs while sharing their opinions. The conflict reminded me that people might not understand my path, and that's okay.

When making difficult choices, listen to your heart as much as your head.

RESPECT IS EARNED

The people you disappoint when you follow your intuition have no choice but to respect your courage in the future. Hard feelings dissolve, and they'll most likely recognize the bravery it took for you to follow your heart instead of pure logic. It will earn you more respect than you can imagine. Two years after I turned down the speaking agency, the individual I'd spoken to on the phone sent me an email saying that he was proud of me.

The life you create is a result of all the choices you make. As Jim Rohn, a self-development teacher, says, success is nothing more than a few simple disciplines, practised every day; while failure is simply a few errors in judgment, repeated every day.

Develop the discipline of listening to and following your intuition, and you'll find it easier to avoid those errors in judgment. When you get overwhelmed, understand that making a decision isn't only a thinking exercise but also a feeling exercise. Whether or not a decision feels right is just as important as whether it makes logical sense. When the pressure of a decision weighs on your shoulders, remember, the dots will connect in your future. The only wrong choice is the one that doesn't align with your intuition, so trust it and follow it, however unreasonable it may appear to yourself and others.

TAKEAWAYS

- Trust your intuition when it's trying to tell you something, and have faith in your decisions. The dots will eventually connect.

- Nobody can tell you that your decisions are right or wrong when it comes to your dreams and goals—they're *your* dreams and goals. Your actions are what determine success or failure.

- Logic isn't enough when it comes to chasing your dreams. Don't just consider whether it makes sense—consider whether it feels right.

- It's often your perception of yourself, and your lack of faith in your intuition, that stops you from following through, not others' opinions.

- The people you disappoint when you follow your intuition have no choice but to respect your courage in the future.

Over the last six chapters, we've looked at beliefs that will move you closer to your dreams. Beliefs are the foundation of all success, and they lead you to an equally important part of the process: actions.

What you believe and what you choose to do about those beliefs are what brings you results. That's why the second section of this book is filled with specific actions you can take to move closer to your dreams and goals. Let's dive in!

PART TWO

ACTIONS

CHAPTER SEVEN

•

COMMIT TO SMALL CONSISTENT ACTIONS

•

Action: Be Consistent

There is no change without time and consistency. The reason most people don't bring their dreams to life is that they lack the patience required to allow time to compound their efforts. We live in a world of instant gratification. We've been taught that it's normal to want something today and receive it tomorrow, and everything we need to survive can be delivered to us in just a few hours or days. We don't even have to leave our houses. This can make it difficult to remain patient and consistent in the pursuit of our dreams—unlike groceries and toilet paper, no one is going to deliver success to our doorsteps tomorrow morning.

WORLD ISSUES CLASS

During my senior year, after my second knee surgery, I was feeling lost. Every day, I'd show up to class on crutches with bandages and ice packs wrapped around my knee to reduce the swelling and heal faster, and I was doing everything in my power to get back on the soccer field. Despite my outward smiles when people asked how I was doing or if they could help, I was exhausted; and, although I hadn't been diagnosed, I knew I was depressed. No one around me knew how much I was struggling to regain and reinvent my identity.

Then, the most amazing teacher entered my life. I walked into his classroom to find him seated with his feet resting on top of his desk. Michael Loudfoot was close to retirement and had this contagious aura of hope. Once all of us students had settled, he stood, walked directly into the middle of the class-room, introduced himself, and said, "Don't believe anything I tell you this semester. If something makes you curious, I want you to go home and verify the facts yourself."

I'll never forget those words. I soon learned that his passion was getting students curious about life, and he believed that curiosity was the starting point of all greatness. He was the teacher who helped me understand that soccer was only one game of thousands that I could play in this world.

He spent most of the semester breaking down the lives of people who radi-cally changed our world. We studied Malala Yousafzai, Martin Luther King Jr., Malcolm X, William Wilberforce, Rosa Parks, Aristotle, and many more. Class would begin the moment Mr. Loudfoot started speaking because everything he had to share was worth taking notes on. I'd never leave fourth period with fewer than three full pages of writing, and every few seconds I'd scan the room and find at least one person shaking out the cramps in their hand. And writing wasn't even mandatory in the class.

After taking us on a journey through the histories of these influential people, Mr. Loudfoot challenged us to identify the characteristics they shared. He believed that if we could see even a small part of ourselves in these people, we could begin to realize how powerful we are. While each of them had many traits that made them unique, they all had one thing in common: they performed thousands of small, consistent actions that led to global changes. Mr. Loudfoot proved to us that if you want to change the world, change your situation, or change your life, you can. **All you have to do is commit to small, consistent actions.**

Those three words stuck with me and changed my perspective. The idea made things feel doable.

We're often afraid to start a new project or chase a dream because it feels out of reach and overwhelming. But all great things are achieved in steps. When you think about your goals through this perspective, the only thing you need to focus on is your next small step.

PLAY A NEW GAME

My teacher's words offered me a challenge and a template for a new "game." For the first time since the age of five, I began carrying a new belief that I didn't have to play soccer to be happy or live a meaningful life—that through my commitment to small, consistent actions, I could build competence in something totally new. On a typical day, after school I'd put on headphones and dance my way home listening to Drake, but the day after that lesson I had two questions running through my mind on a loop: "How am I going to change the world?" and "What is my small, consistent action?"

Two weeks later, I stumbled over the answer—literally. I tripped over a piece of trash on the sidewalk. I passed pieces of litter every day while travelling to and from school, so why I felt the urge to pick up this piece is a mystery, but I did. Realizing that picking up trash was something I was capable of doing, I decided to put my teacher's theory to the test. Every day, I committed to filling a bag of trash on my walk home. It became my small, consistent action for the last four months of my senior year.

There was no plan or vision. I just wanted to see if this action would lead to a big change. Five days before the summer break, I was walking home and picking up trash when my buddy Dillon pulled over in his car, rolled down his window, and asked, "What the heck are you doing?" I explained what Mr. Loudfoot had taught about small, consistent actions leading to massive changes and that, although I didn't know what to do with my life, this was one action I could take to make the world a better place.

Dillon laughed and said, "Let's do something with this!" And that was the dawn of the PickWaste initiative that I talked about in Chapter 4. You wouldn't believe the impact this volunteer initiative created, and the idea was simple: gather people in our community for one hour a week and pick up trash.

The first cleanup was on July 1, 2017. It was just Dillon, two of our friends, and me, and we met up at a beach with gloves and a few garbage bags we stole from our parents. After that first cleanup, we created an Instagram page, where we posted a picture of the trash we collected and invited others to volunteer.

The initiative quickly grew, and our city began supplying us with all the gloves, garbage bags, and permission form templates. They even marketed our program on their main website. Local schools began inviting us to speak and recruit their students as volunteers. Before we knew it, we had a list of over five hundred people receiving emails about future cleanups.

What started as a summer experiment in 2017 never stopped. PickWaste is now an annual event that still occurs in our home city. At the time of writing, we've completed over three hundred cleanups and filled just about three thousand bags of litter. The initiative was featured on the national news, and we provided over six thousand volunteer hours to local high school students. It was the success of this initiative that led me to the work I do today—speaking to youth around North America.

WHAT DO YOU WANT TO CHANGE?

I didn't share the PickWaste story with you in the hope that you'll grab a garbage bag and start filling it with trash—although that's never a bad idea. I shared it to show how small, consistent actions lead to big changes. With patience and consistency, you can bring your dreams to life. So, what's your new small, consistent action? What do you want to change?

Writer Will Durant said, "We are what we repeatedly do. Excellence, then, is not an act, but a habit."[24] Malcolm Gladwell popularized this idea in his best-selling book *Outliers*. His theory states that the journey to mastering anything requires that you invest at least ten thousand hours of deliberate practice in

[24] Will Durant, *The Story of Philosophy: The Lives and Opinions of the Greater Philosophers* (New York: Simon and Schuster, 2009).

it.[25] Listen to the stories of anyone who's achieved notable success and you will find a throughline. Each of them pursued their work and mastered their craft for years before realizing success. Even the people who appear to have become overnight-success stories usually have much more to share when questioned in interviews.

Take *Squid Game*, for example. Its creator, Hwang Dong-Hyuk, wrote the show in 2008 and spent the next ten years pitching his idea without success. Rejection was his only constant. While writing the show, Hwang was in a bad financial situation and had to sell his laptop, which he used to write his show ideas. Fast-forward to 2021, and *Squid Game* was ranked number one in ninety-four countries and was on track to be Netflix's most popular show of all time.[26] After all the rejection he faced, Dong-Hyuk could have easily given up and decided the show wouldn't succeed. After ten years, no one could have told him he hadn't tried. Instead, he remained consistent in action and patient in self-belief, which ultimately resulted in success.

When you're just getting started, remind yourself that consistency is better than perfection. The goal is to consistently hit the publish button on whatever project you're hoping to bring to life. In the field of technology, this idea of creating something, releasing it into the world, and then adjusting, is known as rapid iteration.

---

[25] Malcolm Gladwell, *Outliers: The Story of Success* (Back Bay Books, Little, Brown and Company, 2019).

[26] Frank Pallotta and Liz Kang, "Exclusive: Squid Game Is Netflix's 'Biggest Ever' Series Launch," CNN Business, October 13, 2021, https://www.cnn.com/2021/10/12/media/squid-game-netflix-viewership.

Kanye West provided a unique example of rapid iteration when releasing his 2021 project *Donda*. He lived in a stadium while working on the album and routinely live-streamed the performances of unreleased songs, the removal of scratched vocals, the creation of added verses, and everything in between. Millions of people watched him create the album, which gave him access to feedback from his huge fan base. He repeated this cycle of creating, releasing, and iterating his music before finally publishing his album. Don't allow your desire to be perfect stop you from starting and staying consistent.

SCRAP THE IDEA OF PERFECTION

When I first started pursuing my dream of becoming a speaker, I'd practice my speeches in the shower, reciting my stories to a wall of wet tiles. Sometimes I'd step out of the shower, dripping with water, to read the lines I'd forgotten from my laptop, which was sitting open beside the sink. My parents probably walked by the washroom dozens of times wondering who the heck I was speaking to.

Did those first few speeches suck? Absolutely. Would I be where I am right now if I let my desire to be perfect stop me from getting on stage and speaking? Absolutely not. Again, small, consistent actions are better than perfection.

- Want to lose weight? Start by consistently going for a daily twenty-minute walk.

- Want to save more money? Start by consistently saving 10 percent of each paycheck.

- Want to read more books? Start by consistently reading ten pages every night.

- Want to learn a new skill? Start by consistently carving out small blocks of time each day to work on it.

At the beginning of your journey, you'll have no results to show for your efforts or ideas. It will be easy to get discouraged and give up. What separates those who succeed from those who fail is patience, time, and consistency.

WATERING PAVEMENT

Taking the right action is more important than just taking any action.

Today's culture glorifies staying up all night, disregarding self-care, and placing monetary success at the centre of your life, so many of us believe that working fifteen-hour days is what will bring our dreams to life. It's easy to convince yourself that being busy and "grinding" equates to progress and success, but don't fall into this trap. In Chapter 1, we talked about the idea that not all opinions and beliefs are equal. The same is true for actions.

Being busy doesn't make you successful; working hard on the right things does. Don't get me wrong—you'll be required to make sacrifices, and there will be long days. Just make sure you invest your time and energy in activities that will move you closer to your dreams and goals. Many actions are a waste of time, so you'll need to consistently monitor yourself to determine when you may need a course correction. Mentors and others who've climbed the mountain you wish to scale can also help you ensure you're taking the right actions.

Imagine you go outside a few times a week to water your grass. Your neighbour also goes outside every day, but instead of watering his grass he waters his driveway. While his grass is dying, he boasts that he goes outside every day, sacrificing time with his family to make sure his yard is beautiful. Sure, he's committed to going outside every day, but he's watering the damn pavement! His commitment results in zero progress, yet he continues taking the same action every day. Despite his dead grass and personal frustration, he chooses to celebrate his busyness and dedication.

Do you know someone like this? Someone who's always busy and wears their grind on their shoulder but seems to make nothing happen? This analogy is obviously an exaggeration, but it illustrates why some people never bring their dreams to life. Don't mistake busyness for progress or constant activity for success. Let this analogy remind you that commitment is great, but not when you're committed to the wrong actions.

I've been guilty of "watering the pavement," and if you're honest with yourself, I'm sure you can identify those moments in your life as well. When you realize you're doing it, swallow your pride and turn off the hose. Identify where you're going wrong and recommit yourself to actions that will move you forward. It won't be long before your grass starts growing again.

PRACTICE PATIENCE

Once you find the steps that will bring your dream to life, be patient and buckle up for the long journey. Patience can be the most challenging aspect of chasing your dream; I wish someone had told me when I was in school that you can take all the correct actions and still see no changes.

As a teenager, I was obsessed with lifting weights—more specifically, with having abs. I'd watch the Rocky Balboa boxing movies and listen to the film soundtracks while running laps around the neighbourhood. I'd do hundreds of push-ups and sit-ups, and nothing changed, at least not for a long time. What I didn't understand was that the day you begin going to the gym is not the day your body transforms. Of course, exercising is the right action; but without the compounding effects of time, nothing can change.

During my second year building a speaking career, schools were shut due to COVID-19. Things were difficult, to say the least. When it rains it pours, as the saying goes—and I didn't have an umbrella. Although I was taking lots of action and making difficult choices, it seemed like nothing was changing. Hearing the frustration in my voice, one of my mentors said, "Sam, let me paint you a picture. Imagine you're on a farm planting seeds. Every day you spend hours in the heat planting and watering them while others walk past your farm to buy vegetables from the grocery store. It's difficult because you haven't seen any progress yet, but what you don't understand is that six months from now, you'll have acres of vegetables while the people who walked past you every day will still be shopping at the grocery store."

There are no shortcuts to greatness. My mentor helped me see that patience and consistency are the keys. You aren't supposed to see results right away; if your situation changes instantly, without a change in your mindset due to hard work and appreciation for the process, you'll be unprepared for your success. This is why lottery winners who have bad money habits generally spend all their winnings and return to their average lives within a few years. There's a reason excellence takes ten thousand hours, so don't wish for a shortcut. Instead, figure out the actions you need to take and remain patient.

The step that stops most people is the first one, but all you need to do is take one small step and then focus on the next step in front of you. Over time, with patience and consistency, you will have taken numerous small steps and created massive change. Stop convincing yourself that your idea is too big. Stop convincing yourself that the project will require too much work. Instead, figure out the next smallest action. Once you complete it, move on to the next one.

TAKEAWAYS

- Your small, consistent actions lead to big changes.

- Consistency is better than perfection when you're just getting started.

- Not all actions are equal. Commitment is great, but don't commit yourself to the wrong actions.

- Be patient. You can take all the correct actions and still see no changes because time needs to play its role.

In certain contexts, inaction can be just as important as action. Along your journey, you'll need to stop participating in certain activities, and you'll need to "remove the cookies from the pantry." In the next chapter, we'll explore the concept of sacrifice.

Commitment to small, consistent actions is a way of life—a movement. Use it to reach your goals and change things in your life. Every day I ask myself what small, consistent actions I can take to move one step closer to my dreams. The phrase is written at the top of each page in my journal and on the bracelet that hasn't left my wrist in over three years. I use the hashtag #SmallConsistentActions on all my social media posts and even have the phrase tattooed on me (my mom is not impressed!). If this idea changes your perspective, or your life in any way, please let me know by using the hashtag on social media or by emailing your story to book@samdemma.com.

CHAPTER EIGHT

•

REMOVE THE COOKIES FROM THE PANTRY

•

Action: Make the Sacrifice

There are no cookies in my pantry. Actually, that's usually true, but as I write this a container filled with my grandma's famous cookies is sitting up there—the kind of cookies that you dip in your tea and that melt in your mouth. They're the best. Anyway, this chapter isn't about my obsession with my nonna's cookies or why you should stop eating cookies. This chapter is about making an important decision.

When I was growing up, my parents would fill the shelves of the pantry and fridge with healthy foods. This was partly because my grandparents grew up on farms and didn't give my parents junk food, which taught them to prioritize their health, and partly because I was obsessed with becoming a professional soccer player. Eating well meant I had a better chance of making that dream a reality. I was the kid who wouldn't eat cake or dessert at dinner parties, and whenever my parents brought home junk food we'd get into an argument. By the time I was in high school, these decisions, along with a strict training regimen, had put me in the best physical shape I'd ever been in.

At school, it was a lot more difficult to stay disciplined. During lunch, I'd watch my friends trade snacks with each other. I'd have homemade sandwiches, carrots, celery, and nuts, and everyone around me would pull out Fruit Roll-Ups, chocolate bars, Oreos, and Dunkaroos. No one ever wanted to trade with me. Occasionally I'd treat myself to sushi at the nearby plaza, but more often than not my lunchbox smelled like a garden.

When you're doing something different from everyone around you, you may feel as if you're missing out on something, at least at first. But as time passes, you'll see that all the decisions you made led you to become the person you want to be.

RESET YOUR ENVIRONMENT

Maybe you're thinking that I'm too strict, too hard on myself when it comes to eating a healthy diet; but honestly, deciding to cut out junk food wasn't difficult. I'd been dreaming of playing professional soccer since I was five, and one important aspect of reaching that goal was my health. I'd often ask myself, "What can you do to give yourself the best odds of reaching this goal?" Then I'd go all in. I'd take all the cookies out of the pantry.

The idea is simple, and it has nothing to do with food: stop committing to things and then leaving yourself an easy way to slip back into bad habits. Because when things get tough, your willpower will likely fail.

- If you decide to start eating a healthy diet, throw out all the junk food in your pantry.

- If you decide to stop using social media, delete all the apps from your phone.

- If you decide to go to sleep at 9:00 p.m., leave your electronics outside your bedroom.

- If you decide to stop playing video games, sell your console—now.

DESTROY THE CIGARETTES

When we were younger, my sister, our cousins, and I wanted to get our grandfather to stop smoking cigarettes. As we grew up, our concern for his health increased. We knew his bad habit would likely lead to lung cancer, and the second-hand smoke wasn't good for anyone.

One summer, while we were all at the family cottage, we made a serious attempt to convince our grandfather to stop smoking once and for all. While he was fishing, we snuck into his minivan, grabbed his five packs of cigarettes, cut each cigarette into tiny pieces, and then burned them all. We hid the remains underneath the ashes of our bonfire pit. When he returned to grab a pack, let's just say he was really upset. He proceeded to chase me around the cottage with a pitchfork—true story! Cutting out junk food from your diet doesn't seem too extreme now, does it?

Although this didn't convince our grandfather to stop smoking, we thought it was a great attempt. Contrary to popular opinion, when it comes to making changes cold turkey is always my first choice.

Emptying your pantry and destroying your cigarettes are actions you need to take on the path to creating a meaningful life. So, be honest with yourself: where are you playing it safe and not wholeheartedly committing to the process? There are probably obvious actions you can identify in an instant, but often the things we need to remove the most are buried well below the surface. And sometimes they disguise themselves as a safety net.

"SAFETY" IS HOLDING YOU BACK

The Dark Knight Rises is one of my favourite DC movies. There's a scene where Batman gets sent to "the pit"—a prison from which only one person had ever escaped. Imagine a giant well, without the water. The walls are made of stone, and the only way out is to scale the ledges that protrude from the walls.

The other prisoners tell Batman that nearly everyone who tried the climb failed due to a gap between two stone ledges. He tries jumping from one to the other a few times, with a rope tied to his waist to prevent him from falling to his death, and he fails. Then, a prisoner tells him that the only way he'll succeed is to make the jump without the rope. The prisoner explains that fear is one of the strongest motivators, and attempting the jump without the rope will give Batman the adrenalin needed to surpass his body's normal capabilities. So, Batman tries this, and, spoiler alert, he succeeds.[27]

---

[27] *The Dark Knight Rises*, directed by Christopher Nolan (2012; Warner Bros. Pictures, 2012), accessed June 20, 2022.

The rope that kept him safe ended up being the thing that held him back. Do you have any ropes like this in your life? If so, it's time to cut them loose and use your adrenalin.

I know this isn't easy. When I started my business, I spent two years working part-time at a restaurant to support myself until the business took off. I told myself that once things started working out, I'd leave. I kept delaying quitting that job, and if it weren't for the global pandemic it might have taken me a few more years to cut that rope.

Things began exploding in my business and life (in a good way) once I left the restaurant. In hindsight, that job wasn't keeping me safe—it was holding me back. Most of your safety ropes aren't keeping you safe either. They're strangling you while making you too comfortable. They're delaying the process you know you need to start to get to where you want to go. Your idea of safety is often an iilusion, so stop playing it safe.

NO MORE ALCOHOL

Recently, I decided that on every birthday I'd remove something from my life that could be holding me back. These decisions usually seem extreme to others, but that's okay because it's my life. On September 11, 2021—my twenty-second birthday—I decided I wouldn't take one sip of alcohol for a whole year.

I don't drink alcohol often, but whenever I do I always feel like garbage for a few days afterward. So I asked myself, "Why would you put something in your body that you know is going to make you feel terrible? Not only that, but it takes a few days to fully recover, and you do this a dozen times a year, so you end up throwing away so many days that you could have used to make progress on your dreams."

For the longest time, I believed that to have fun I had to be a little tipsy. Honestly, it was just an excuse for not putting myself out there because I was worried that people would judge me for being me. But every situation is what you make of it. Period. I know that drinking in moderation is okay, but this was something I was genuinely excited to remove from my life. The decision was inspired by the following social media post by rapper Jack Harlow:

> Haven't had a single sip of alcohol in 2021. Going the rest of the year without it. Maybe I'll never take another sip, who knows? My favorite vice was definitely drinking (I don't like to smoke) but if I learned anything this year it's that I don't need it. I don't usually say a lot in my captions because it feels like anything worth telling y'all I should just put in my songs . . . but today felt like a good time for a life update. I'm really grateful for how far we've come and I want you to know I appreciate all of you. But I'm hungrier right now than I've ever been. I'm prepared to become a well-oiled machine to take this s*** to the next level. See you soon.[28]

What an inspiration. This post moved me because I know how it feels to sacrifice something in the pursuit of a dream and goal. Like Jack and anyone else who has achieved greatness, you must be willing to become a well-oiled machine to take your life to the next level.

Another inspiration for my decision was Curtis Jackson, better known as 50 Cent. Contrary to popular belief and his own song lyrics, 50 rarely drinks and never smokes. He disclosed in his book *Hustle Harder, Hustle Smarter* and

---

[28] Jack Harlow (@jackharlow), Instagram photo, posted August 15, 2021, accessed June 20, 2022, https://www.instagram.com/p/CSm7AdvLQk7/.

in interviews that he largely refrains from drinking—even his own brand of liquor! He may take a few sips when he's with company, but after one drink he has the server swap out the alcohol for Canada Dry.[29]

When you give up something in pursuit of your dreams, at some point in your future that sacrifice will show up as progress.

New opportunities might not look exactly like you expected, but they *will* present themselves to you. Years spent playing soccer and avoiding junk food, parties, and video games helped me develop discipline, time-management, accountability, and a strong work ethic. These qualities, built through sacrifice, are the reason I succeed today in business. I can't tell you what your safety ropes and vices are, but I can tell you that if you decide to remove those things, right now, your life will begin to change.

Name one thing you could remove from your life to make it better. I invite you to get rid of that thing—right now.

When you start being more intentional about your actions, taking responsibility for your results, and going all in by cutting safety ropes loose and removing vices, things will change. If this sounds a little extreme, good. Only those willing to push the boundaries and live life in the extremes will make an impact worth remembering. So, stop waiting, and start taking the cookies off your shelf.

---

[29] Ian Mohr, "50 Cent Avoids Drinking His Own Champagne in the Club," *Page Six*, April 14, 2020, https://pagesix.com/2020/04/14/50-cent-avoids-drinking-his-own-champagne-in-the-club/.

TAKEAWAYS

- If you're feeling and doing things that are different from everyone else, you're not missing out—you're building your unique story and personality.

- When you decide to make a positive change, don't give yourself an easy way to slip back into bad habits.

- Stop playing it safe—your idea of safety is probably an illusion.

- When you give up something in the pursuit of your dreams, that sacrifice will eventually show up as progress.

One of the special things that makes you *you* is your creativity. Emptying your pantry will help you tap into your creative genius. As kids, we tap into our imaginations dozens of times a day, but as we age we often turn off our imaginative impulses and dismiss them as weird. The next chapter will re-awaken you to the importance of your creativity and remind you to appreciate your ideas—they're powerful!

CHAPTER NINE

•

ACT ON
YOUR IDEAS

•

Action: Get Creative

Hey Colm, I'm driving from Toronto to Brooklyn on Feb 5th in the hope
that we can chat about this idea face-to-face. Really looking forward to
hearing from you.

I pasted these words at the bottom of a website I'd spent over twenty hours
building to pitch an idea to Colm Dillane, aka KidSuper, a well-known designer
who's been disrupting the fashion industry for over fifteen years. His authentic style and unique eye for design have helped him land partnerships with big
brands and opportunities at some of the world's largest fashion shows. When
he started his brand, only he and his friends wore his clothes, but today you
can see them on many A-list celebrities.

I wanted to collaborate with him on creating the Empty Backpack—a backpack for dreamers and independent thinkers. It was just past midnight when I

finished watching one of Colm's interviews on YouTube.[30] My legs were shaking with excitement due to an idea sparked from his words. I planned to drive to his store in New York to pitch him the idea in person.

The challenge was that Colm Dillane knew nothing about me, we have zero mutual connections, and he's incredibly busy working with some of the biggest artists on the planet. Rather than allowing the little voice in my mind to stop me from acting, I leaned into my creativity and brought an idea to life. (I know you've also had conversations with that little voice that tries to silence your creativity. Don't let it stop you.)

My idea had two parts. First, I'd build a website to share my collaboration idea. Second, I'd get Colm's attention so he'd actually see the website. I scoured the internet to learn everything I could about Colm and the KidSuper brand. The more I learned about him, the more my imagination started filling my mind with ideas.

WHAT IF?

One of the most interesting things I learned was that Colm had an M&M's vending machine door in the basement of his clothing store. It served as the entrance to a music studio, and people wouldn't leave his store without taking a picture beside the bright yellow door. I chuckled when I learned about it, and my imagination planted an idea in my mind. "What if you found a way to use a vending machine door on the loading page of the website you build for him?"

Creativity is one of your most valuable assets. Acting on your "what if" ideas can create huge opportunities and impact. In the future, robots might take

---

[30] Hello Creatively, "KidSuper teaches Building a Brand," April 1, 2021, YouTube video, https://www.youtube.com/watch?v=cXJURralLvl.

over our physical work, but it will be a long time, if ever, before scientists can program them to be creative in the same ways that humans are. Even if this happens, your creative ideas will still place you in a category of one because you are unique and there will only ever be one of you. Your imagination is your greatest advantage. It's no accident that ideas are called "intellectual property"—they hold serious value.

Not only did I follow through on that creative idea (kidsuper.samdemma.com), but I also shipped Colm a package of M&M's from which I'd removed the candy and inserted a sheet of paper with the website URL and password on it. I taped a yellow M&M's wrapper to the white envelope and prayed that it would reach him.

Colm never received the package, but the image of the yellow door eventually caught his attention. I shared everything with him on Instagram, and after reviewing the website he was kind enough to let me know he wouldn't be in New York when I planned to drive down, and we've since exchanged many messages. Although the collaboration hasn't happened yet, I'm certain we'll work together at some point. It was my imagination that brought this idea and story to life, so stop discounting yours.

Look around you. Everything you see was once an idea in someone's head. Whatever you're sitting on while you read this book started as an idea and is now impacting your life. Ideas transcend time and space; your ideas can influence someone hundreds of years from now—but only if you bring them to life.

OWN YOUR CREATIVITY

Someone who constantly reminds people of the importance of creativity is platinum rapper, singer, and producer Russ. Listen to any of his interviews and you'll hear him talk about ownership in the music industry.[31] He explains that record labels make most of their money from their artists' streams, not from tours. When the music—someone's creative expression—is great, the labels make money. There's no tour without the music. In that industry, if you don't understand the power of owning your creativity, you may sign an agreement that forces you to hand over all your ideas in return for an amount of money that can seem large but is only a fraction of their true value. This can be compared to someone putting you in golden handcuffs.

Russ is one of the only artists I know who passionately encourages people to own their creative ideas and who openly shares pictures of his weekly earnings on social media to prove how powerful this choice can be. Some weeks, his music generates him over US$100,000.[32] His creative ideas made him wealthy, and yours can do the same for you. Whether you're an aspiring artist or could care less about music is irrelevant; what matters is that you value your creativity. Your ideas are your greatest assets—never let someone take them from you.

CREATIVITY IS ACCESSIBLE

I have some good news for you: **Creativity isn't something you're born with—it's something you make time for.** Sitting down and dedicating chunks of time for creative thinking leads to ideas, and discipline is one of the main ingredients of creative output. In a world of constant distraction, it's easy to fall into the trap of consuming rather than creating. People often miss

---

[31] Jay Shetty Podcast, "Russ ON: Delusional Self-Confidence & How to Start Manifesting Your Dream Life," May 3, 2021, YouTube video, 57:48, https://www.youtube.com/watch?v=-4c61A2VD8k.

[32] Bruce Houghton, "Russ Earns $100K Weekly As TuneCore Artist, Offers Advice to Others," Hypebot, November 11, 2020, https://www.hypebot.com/hypebot/2020/11/russ-earns-100k-weekly-as-tunecore-artist-offers-advice-to-others.html.

out on the benefits of their creativity simply because they don't make time for their imaginations to wander.

As a kid, I'd run through the forest in our backyard creating pretend worlds and fighting invisible armies. My cousins and I dreamed up an imaginary martial arts school that we called Ninja Fighting School, and we would spend hours throwing around green coasters, aka, deadly ninja stars. If one touched you, you had to play dead and wait for someone to revive you. When we're young, we seem wired to use our imaginations, but somewhere along the way we just stop. We stop making time for those magical moments and dismiss fictional ideas as a waste of time.

Instead of allowing our imaginations to wander, we "grow up" and fill our schedule with "realistic" pursuits, forgetting about the power of our imagination. If that's not sad enough, we usually spend any free time we do have indulging in distractions. There's nothing wrong with scrolling on social media or watching Netflix, but what if you spent some of that time validating your creative ideas? What if you devoted some energy to walking through the forest or to sitting in silence with just a pen and a notepad?

One of your small, consistent actions moving forward could be to spend ten to fifteen minutes every day in a physical space and mindset that allows your imagination to wander. Discipline yourself, carve out the time, and you'll soon realize that you can access creativity.

YOUR MENLO PARK

If you want to get creative, start by finding a distraction-free space. When it comes to this idea, there's no better teacher than Thomas Edison. By the time he died, Edison had amassed a record 1,093 patents.[33] Because of Edison's creative contributions, you can use a lightbulb to stay up late and finish an essay, a telephone to call your friends, and a video camera to capture your favourite moments. Edison changed our lives with this creativity.

Everyone praises Edison for his inventions, but what's less known is where he worked on them. Menlo Park is now a museum, but once it was a large laboratory within a warehouse space in New Jersey. Edison and his team built it to create an environment where they could work in isolation, and he claimed to have had his best ideas while working in this space. Maybe you're like me and can't afford a warehouse, but we can all create or find a space that's inspiring and distraction free. For me, Menlo Park is a small office in the basement of my parents' house. In the next section, I'll tell you about one recent idea born in the silence of that space.

WHEN THEY ZIG, YOU ZAG

Shortly after the initial COVID-19 outbreak, I discovered Charlie Rocket. You may have seen TikToks or Instagram stories about his work with the Dream Machine; he and his team drove around America in a painted RV making people's dreams come true. One of his most well-known projects was with a painter named Richard Hutchins. Within three weeks of finding this man on the streets, Charlie and his team helped him turn his dream of becoming a professional artist into a reality. They raised over US$200,000 selling his art online and managed to get the attention and support of several celebrities, including Oprah, Will Smith, and Steve Harvey.[34]

---

[33] History.com Editors, "Thomas Edison," History.com, original November 9, 2009, updated June 6, 2019, https://www.history.com/topics/inventions/thomas-edison.

[34] Abbey Clark, "How This Homeless Artist Became a Viral Internet Sensation," CNN Style, August 9, 2021, https://www.cnn.com/style/article/richard-hutchins-homeless-artist/index.html.

I discovered Charlie and his team months before they helped Richard Hutchins, and I immediately imagined a unique collaboration with them. While they drove from city to city making people's dreams come true, I could speak at the local high schools about their work to spread the initiative on the ground. I'd spent the past three years doing this same work on my own—this could be a chance to do it as part of a team working toward a common goal. The thought gave me goosebumps and a wild amount of energy. When you can't go a day without thinking about an idea, it's worth pursuing.

A few months passed, and that idea developed into an obsession. It got to a point where I couldn't sleep at night. Every day I'd tell my parents, "I'm going to work with Charlie and the Dream Team." I'd write in my journal, *Charlie and I are working together, he just doesn't know it yet.* From the outside looking in, I probably sounded outrageous. People around me were most likely thinking, "Cool, but Sam, how are you going to get his attention, let alone establish a partnership?"

That was the challenge. Thousands of people were messaging Charlie each day pitching ideas and collaborations. Why would he care about a kid from another country blowing up his phone? This is the kind of situation that requires creativity. To win over the attention of an extraordinary person, you need to be confident enough to believe you deserve a seat at their table and then creative enough in your outreach to cut through the noise and make an impression.

Marketing expert Seth Godin calls these strategic ideas purple cows.[35] Imagine you're driving in a rural community surrounded by fields filled with cows.

---

[35] Seth Godin, *Purple Cow: Transform Your Business by Being Remarkable* (London: Penguin, 2005).

If you were to see a purple cow among hundreds of black-and-white ones, would it grab your attention?

Absolutely! It's so unique that you can't help but look. You don't have to paint yourself purple, but unless you show up in a unique and remarkable way you'll struggle to sell your idea.

The idea is simple: when other people zig, you zag. And so, instead of messaging Charlie, like thousands of other people did, I decided I'd send him something in the mail. I didn't have his mailing address, but I was determined to figure that out later.

I listened to every one of his sixty-two podcast episodes and took a page of notes on each; that took me over three weeks. I then stapled the sixty-two pages together like a book and created a cover page that read, "Hey Charlie, my onboarding is done. When can we get started?" The final page in the booklet had a URL, which contained a video for him and his team.

The next question that ran through my mind was: "What could I send that would make the package stand out?" Again, creativity rose to the occasion. I found a website that helped me create a custom pizza box with Charlie's face and branding plastered all over it. At $180, it was the most expensive cardboard box I've ever purchased. But I knew it would have the same effect as seeing a purple cow on a farm.

Success requires boldness. Belief and confidence are contagious, and you must develop extraordinary belief in yourself before others will believe in you. Instead of telling someone how great you are, allow your actions to communicate that message. If you don't think you deserve a seat at the table, you won't take extraordinary action.

With my box and book completed, the next step was to figure out Charlie's mailing address. To be honest, this step seemed impossible because public figures often make it difficult to reach them for safety reasons. Luckily, I knew someone who worked with Charlie, but I hesitated to ask him for the information because I didn't want him to think I was using him to access Charlie. After spending some quiet time thinking, I came up with another creative idea. What if I interviewed someone on Charlie's team, told them the idea, and then asked them for the mailing address?

A mentor of mine once explained that people buy people, products, and services, in that order. For someone to invest in your idea, they need to like you first, and one of the most effective ways to build a relationship with someone is to talk to them. Even better, give them an opportunity to talk about themselves and the things they love.

Please don't get me wrong—there's a difference between genuine curiosity and using people as a step in your strategy. Never confuse the two because the latter will often lead to failure and a ruined reputation. After researching people on the team, I came across the co-founder. His journey piqued my interest and after listening to a few previous interviews of his, I reached out. We had an amazing conversation on my podcast, and at the end of the Zoom interview I explained the idea, held up the decked-out pizza box, and asked for the mailing address. His mind was blown, and he instantly texted me the address. He said it was the most creative way someone had ever reached out to them. That afternoon, I shipped the box to LA.

While all this was going on, the dream team were taking applications for six new full-time positions. To apply, you had to answer a dozen questions on a Google form, and just over two hundred people filled out applications. Without filling out the application, I landed a FaceTime call with the team. My pizza box helped me cut through the noise.

We talked for over an hour, and they told me that I was the only applicant who'd sent something above and beyond the application—the only person who'd used their creativity and imagination when reaching out. The collaboration didn't happen because they weren't looking to bring on another speaker, but I still made a heck of an impression and built some cool relationships, so it was a success in that respect. Knowing when to stop pursuing a dream, collaboration, or opportunity can be difficult. It's a personal decision, although letting go can be just as important as persisting. This "no" from the dream team was one that I wholeheartedly accepted and felt at peace with. Develop the self-awareness to recognize when to get creative and when to let go.

Be persistent, consistent, and creative—one of your ideas will catch on, sending you on the journey of a lifetime.

TAKEAWAYS

- Creativity is one of your most valuable assets. Acting on your "what if" ideas can create huge opportunities and impact.

- Everything around you started as an idea. Your ideas can influence someone hundreds of years from now, but only if you have discipline and bring them to life.

- Creativity isn't something you're born with—it's something you make time for. Dedicate time to letting your imagination wander and you, too, will generate creative ideas.

- People buy people, products, and services in that order. If you want someone to invest in your creative idea, they need to buy into you first.

- Cultivate the discipline to set aside time to come up with creative ideas, and use them to bring your dreams to life. Use them to stand out.

- Look at what everyone else is doing and find with a creative way to do the opposite.

Your creativity has the power to open doors and start conversations you never thought possible. It can help you patent over a thousand things before you die, generate one hundred thousand dollars a week, win the attention of a celebrity, or land you a new job.

You may not know how to build a website or have $180 to buy a pizza box—
that's okay. Creativity is less about having resources and more about being
resourceful. In the next chapter, we'll explore resourcefulness and making
something from nothing. Buckle up!

CHAPTER TEN

•

MAKE SOMETHING FROM NOTHING

•

Action: Tap Into Your Resourcefulness

At sixteen years old, I walked into my dad's office on a mission. I wanted to purchase workout equipment to build a home gym in our basement. It was still my dream to play professional soccer, and I knew I'd have better odds of becoming a pro if I had a gym in the house. As a high-level athlete, you control your physical fitness. The small, consistent actions you take every day affect your fitness on the field.

You should have seen the excitement on my dad's face after I asked him for a home gym. Most students ask their parents for video games or permission to go to a friend's party, and here I was pleading for exercise equipment. Unfortunately, our excitement quickly vanished after browsing a few online stores, when we realized that my gym would cost thousands of dollars. I played soccer five times a week after school, so I couldn't take on a part-time job, and my dad wasn't willing to pay for the gym. Instead, he challenged me. "Find a way to pay for the equipment, and I'll help you pick it up and put it together."

This challenge was a gift. It taught me a lesson that will serve me for the rest of my life—**your circumstances don't determine your success if you're willing to be resourceful.**

Resourcefulness is a prerequisite for bringing any dream to life. Right now, you may not have the money, knowledge, or circumstances you think you need to get what you want. You're not alone. Some of the world's most fulfilled and successful individuals started with little to nothing and grew up in situations that were heartbreaking and traumatic. To make something out of nothing, you must be resourceful. You must leverage what you have and think outside the box.

Being resourceful means persisting until you find a way, even when the goal seems out of reach. Imagine that you're on a road trip that takes you down a narrow highway. The first half of your drive is straightforward and smooth, but then you approach a giant rock in the middle of the highway. The challenge of the rock blocking the highway presents you with two options: turn back and drive home, or be resourceful and find a way to move the rock or get around it. Instead of turning around, maybe you take the jack out of your car and pry the stone off the road. Maybe you convince the next fifty people who drive up to the rock to get out of their cars to help you push it. If you choose to accept the challenge and be resourceful, you won't just reach your goal—you'll also create a pathway that other people can benefit from.

SALVATORE'S GRASS-CUTTING SERVICE

Being resourceful isn't about getting more tools but about finding creative ways to make the most of the ones you already have. One tool that no one can ever take from you is your mind—remember, it's full of creative ideas. For sixteen-year-old Sam, resourcefulness meant creating Salvatore's Grass-Cutting Service, a lawn-care company I thought would earn me the money needed to purchase the gym equipment. (My real name is Salvatore, and I thought it would sound more legitimate than Sam in the business name.)

I printed over a hundred flyers and spent hours walking door to door dropping them in every mailbox on my street. The flyer read:

Hi, my name is Salvatore Demma. I'm sixteen years old, currently in high school and aspire to become a professional soccer player. Due to my busy schedule, no companies will take me on as an employee. Therefore, I am taking it into my own hands and trying to create my own opportunities to support myself as I get older. I am extremely hardworking and can be very flexible to your schedule. I will cut your grass—front and back—for a price that together we deem fair. Because I can't drive, if you live a fair distance away I will use your machine and gas for a reduced cost. I currently have a few customers on your street and would love to gain your business. I guarantee you will not be disappointed! Please consider giving me a chance this year.

This effort resulted in three customers. Two were on my street and the third was a fifteen-minute bike ride away. It wasn't much, but making any amount of money gave me enough inspiration and hope to keep me going. I always made sure to overdeliver to keep the customers happy, but within months summer ended and the city was covered in snow, so I started shovelling for money. While doing that, I came up with another idea that wasn't weather dependent—buying and selling gym equipment online.

RUSTY PILE OF GOLD

Since I was interested in buying a home gym, I thought it would be worthwhile to study online equipment stores to educate myself on pricing. I'd spend fifteen minutes in the morning, fifteen minutes during lunch, and another fifteen minutes after school looking for new listings on eBay, Craigslist, and Kijiji and taking notes on how much things were selling for. Within a few weeks, I could understand when something was a rip-off or a hot deal, and I was ready to get in the game. The process was simple—whenever I noticed something valuable that was underpriced, I'd purchase it, clean it up, and resell it for a profit.

Back then, one pound of steel was valued at about one dollar; so, if someone was selling their weights for less than one dollar per pound, I could confidently purchase them, knowing I'd make a profit. Every few weeks, I'd find something small and make fifty to one hundred dollars. I kept all the cash in a shoebox in my closet (shoutout to Nike for my cardboard-box safe). I'm sure no one would have ever found the stash in the orange box with GYM MONEY written all over it.

Six months into this hustle, I came across a listing that changed everything. A woman was moving out of a house about an hour's drive from mine and wanted to clear out her entire basement gym. The pictures she posted were terrible; the plates were covered in rust and probably hadn't been used in years. She also mentioned that whoever wanted to purchase the equipment would have to disassemble it and carry it out of her basement.

The exciting part was that this woman was willing to sell everything for five hundred dollars. To most people, this listing looked like junk. No one trusts terrible photos online or wants to buy rusted weights, but sometimes being resourceful means taking someone's trash and turning it into treasure. Despite the rusted weights, the terrible photos, and the long drive I'd have to make, I was knowledgeable enough to know this offer had serious value.

The listing included five hundred pounds of weight plates, dumbbells ranging from five to fifty pounds, a squat rack, a bench, a treadmill, a few barbells, and some interlocking floor mats. You may not know what half of those things are, and that's okay. All you need to know is that this would be my largest and last flip. Thankfully, my dad followed through on his promise to help me pick up the equipment. Once we arrived, he was pretty pissed off—he had no idea what he'd committed to because I never explained that it would take over three hours of cranking wrenches and walking up a narrow staircase to get everything into his truck.

Back home, I unloaded everything into the garage, and for the next week you could find me hunched over the workshop table scraping the rust off the equipment with an iron brush. I used silver spray paint to give the equipment a brand-new look, and, piece by piece, I relisted everything online. Within four weeks, the garage was empty and I'd made a profit of $2,500! Finally, with the Nike shoebox containing all the money I needed, I was ready to make a trip to the nearby exercise store. I purchased everything I wanted, and the gym my dad and I assembled in the basement still exists today. I use it every morning before starting my workday.

When I began trying to get a home gym, I had no money and no part-time job, but no one could have told me that it wasn't possible. I was patient enough to understand that reaching this goal would take time, and I was persistent and resourceful in my pursuit. You don't have to know all the steps that will take you from point A to point B. When embarking on a journey to a meaningful life, no one knows the challenges that will occur, and some of them will be out of your control. What *is* in your control is the decision to remain persistent and resourceful.

"CAN'T" IS THE ENEMY OF RESOURCEFULNESS

In Chapter 3, we talked about the importance of redefining the word *no*. Other people will often say this word when rejecting your ideas or projecting their limiting beliefs onto you. The word *can't*, on the other hand, usually comes from your own limiting beliefs and doubtful self-talk. When you use that word, you're placing a ceiling on your possibilities. Choosing resourcefulness means removing that word from your personal vocabulary.

Instead of telling yourself you can't, ask yourself what's required. Trailblaze a path to your desired outcome.

Resourceful people don't wait for the perfect conditions or permission from others to act. Take Ermias Asghedom, for example. At the age of twelve, Ermias, now better known as Nipsey Hussle, received a computer, and he used it to start making music. Unfortunately, the computer broke down and couldn't be used anymore. It was a tragic setback for the young dreamer who had few tools to bring his music to life, but instead of giving up he began reading and studying computer magazines. "I'm gonna build a computer," he told people. Everyone thought he was in over his head.[36]

Imagine a twelve-year-old, in 1997, telling you he was going to build a computer, from scratch, armed with only broken parts and a few magazines. But

---

[36] Rob Kenner, *The Marathon Don't Stop: The Life and Times of Nipsey Hussle* (New York: ATRIA, 2022).

day after day, Ermias persisted with resourceful action. He'd bring home new parts and scatter them on his bedroom floor. It took him only a few weeks to build a fully functional computer, on which he recorded some of his initial music. His family's and friends' minds were blown.

Ermias's story is the perfect example of resourcefulness. He had no idea how to build a computer before he began reading those magazines, but he didn't use the word *can't*, and he wasn't going to be told that he couldn't do it. He knew why he needed the computer and was willing to learn whatever was required to fix it. When you figure out *what* you want and *why* you want it, with enough persistence and resourceful action the *how* figures itself out.

A REMINDER ABOUT PATIENCE

Resourcefulness may also require patience. We discussed the importance of patience in Chapter 7, and, in a world centred around instant gratification, it's important to reiterate how central it is to achieving your dreams.

Patience isn't the opposite of resourcefulness; they're complementary skills. You don't get to choose when things work out, and the timing of your success is outside your control. It took me two years working at a restaurant to build the financial reserve and courage to move full time into business. Earning the money to purchase the gym equipment took a lot longer than expected. Patience is an aspect of resourcefulness and your dream might require an investment of two days, two weeks, or ten years.

Dwelling on things you can't change is the quickest way to make yourself anxious and overwhelmed. Instead, get crystal clear on what you want and why you need it, then take resourceful action and practice patience.

PARKING, PLEASE

Before I started university, I had my own "rock in the middle of the highway" moment. Driving my nonna's SUV to school meant that I'd need a place to park, and it would cost over $800 a year just to park my car in the school parking lot. I decided there had to be a better way and started exercising that resourcefulness muscle. I set out on a journey through the neighbourhood, knocking on doors to see if someone would allow me to rent a space on their driveway for the school year. I even drafted a "driveway parking agreement" that couldn't have been legally enforceable but helped legitimize my request.

I pitched my idea to over fifty homeowners before I finally received a yes. You should have seen the looks on my friends' faces when I told them I was paying half the cost of the school parking fees and that the parking spot was directly across the street from the main building on campus.

Your success isn't determined by what you have or how talented you are. There are people like Ermias, who started with absolutely nothing and went on to create remarkable lives. Your resourcefulness, your willingness to be relentless and do whatever it takes, is what determines your success. So, the next time someone tells you that you can't do something, look them in their eye and say, "Don't tell me I can't—show me what's required."

TAKEAWAYS

- Your circumstances don't determine your success if you're willing to be resourceful.

- Sometimes being resourceful means taking someone's trash and turning it into treasure.

- Remove the word *can't* from your vocabulary.

- Resourceful people don't wait for the perfect conditions or others' permission to take action—they ask what's required.

- Dwelling on things you can't change leads to overwhelm and anxiety. Instead, decide what you want and why you need it, then take resourceful action and practice patience.

Don't mistake resourcefulness and persistence for being harsh or pushy. It's important that your actions don't negatively affect the people around you. In the next chapter, we'll talk about something that consistently gives back to the people who selflessly give it away—kindness.

CHAPTER ELEVEN

•

BE SOMEONE'S TACO

•

Action: Serve Others

There's almost nothing I wouldn't do to spend a few more minutes with Nonno Sam. My grandfather's warm smile, sincere laugh, and giving nature are etched into my memory. Relationships weren't something he took for granted, and he understood that family wasn't defined by blood but by how we choose to treat one another. My grandfather's parents gave him up at birth, and a family with the last name Demma took him in.

Kindness isn't a buzzword I ever heard my grandfather say, but his actions proved it was one of his core values. Even during his final days while battling lung cancer, he'd go out of his way to make sure his family was laughing and having a good time. One day, we were sitting on the carpet in his living room and he removed his dentures and folded the skin of his lips inside his mouth to get a reaction out of us. Every time he did this, my sister, my cousins, and I would burst out laughing.

There was never a shortage of laughs and stories at the dinner table. Nonno Sam had arrived in Canada from Italy with no material possessions, but he lived a rich life filled with values, principles, and service to others. When his kids were growing up, he didn't have time to watch them play sports or follow their dreams, so when he became a grandfather he took great pride in watching his grandchildren pursue their passions.

He'd jump at the opportunity to drive us to dance recitals and soccer, baseball, and hockey games. He'd sit on the sidelines in his green camouflage hunting chair, watching in silence. Although he said few words, you could tell his heart was warm when he spent time with his family.

Of all the lessons my grandfather left me, one sticks like glue. His actions taught me that **some of the most meaningful experiences in life come from being of service to others.** It's one of the few win-win-win experiences life has to offer. When you serve others, you directly benefit because you feel good about yourself. The person you help also benefits from your actions, and the world as a whole becomes a slightly better place because those who benefit are more likely to pay it forward. It starts a positive ripple effect.

Your definition of success may have nothing to do with positively affecting people, and that's okay—but along your journey it's important that your actions don't have the opposite impact and bring others down.

Something that used to stop me from being of service was the belief that my actions had to be big and solve global problems for me to make a difference.

Over time, I learned that you don't have to change the world to change one person's world; a little time, energy, and intention are all it takes to make someone feel appreciated. Despite working two jobs and rarely being home, Nonno Sam did this all the time.

Today, I refer to the idea of going out of your way to make someone else feel special as "being someone's taco."

TACOS FOR DINNER

Do you remember how you felt at the beginning of the COVID-19 pandemic? If you're anything like me, you probably experienced doubt, uncertainty, fear, depression, and anxiety. You were locked in your home, told you couldn't see family or friends, and forced to attend school through a screen. My dream of speaking at conferences, schools, and associations was just beginning to come to life when the pandemic swept the globe and shut down in-person events for the next two years. Within two weeks, I had to cancel over thirty engagements and went through a period of extreme anxiety.

Knowing that I wasn't the only one experiencing difficulties, I called my friends, one by one, to check in and make sure they were doing okay. My first call was to my friend Andrew. Andrew and his wife, Emily, run a phenomenal production company in Toronto. Their company was the first one I ever hired to film my speeches, and I can't recommend them enough.[37]

It was 2:00 p.m. when Andrew picked up the phone to tell me he was still in bed. The pandemic was hurting his business and his mental health, and

---

[37] *Stature Films* is the amazing production company that helped me create my first speaking demo reel.

the tone of voice alone told me he wasn't doing great. Once our phone call ended, I asked myself: *What small action can you take to make Andrew feel a little bit better?*

When I'm down, one thing that makes me feel better is food—not only for the obvious reasons, but also because it's typically accompanied by conversation and laughs. (My PO box is listed at the end of the book, and I won't be upset if you send me some food. Just saying.) And so, my first task was to figure out what Andrew and Emily liked eating. The mission had begun. I scoured Facebook for any post Andrew might have made about food he liked. I scrolled all the way back to October 2019 and finally found a comment: "My #vote is tacos for dinner."

Okay, who doesn't love tacos? This will sound weird, but please stop reading right now—yes, in the middle of this story—and take a moment to randomly spam someone you love with taco emojis. Heck, if you want to make me laugh, go ahead and fill my direct messages on Instagram (@Sam_Demma) with taco emojis.

Now knowing that Andrew and Emily loved tacos, I purchased a taco dinner for two (soft shells, of course) through Uber Eats and included a note for the delivery person that read, "Please let Andrew and Emily know this is from Sam and he hopes they feel better." I hoped the tacos would lift their spirits and save them the time and energy of cooking a meal. I then sat at the base of my staircase like a child waiting for their family to wake up on their birthday, watching the driver's progress on my phone.

At 6:29 p.m. my phone vibrated with a notification that the tacos had arrived. Less than a minute later, I got a FaceTime call from Andrew and Emily. They were sitting in their kitchen with the box of tacos open behind them on the countertop. Both had broad smiles on their faces and tears running down their cheeks. They told me that they'd never forget this moment and couldn't stress how much it meant to them during this difficult period.

A taco dinner for two changed how my friends felt and created a joyful memory. From that day forward, Andrew wouldn't stop spamming my phone with taco emojis. So seriously, go spam someone. That holiday season, as a surprise, Andrew and Emily hired a designer to create a cute smiling taco with the phrase "Be Someone's Taco" above it. They encouraged me to share this story to encourage others to be someone's taco.

As a result, thousands of kind acts have occurred, and hundreds of people walk this planet with smiling taco shirts that help spark conversations about serving others. "Be someone's taco" has grown into a movement. Taco Bell Canada jumped on board; at select schools where I give speeches, they provide students with free taco coupons in exchange for performing small acts of kindness.[38]

Do you remember the last time someone made you feel special and appreciated? Every day, you have the opportunity to give that feeling to someone else. It's not about buying people tacos, of course (though who doesn't love tacos?)—it's about using your talents to make a positive difference in the lives of those around you. You and I can be someone's taco every single

---

[38] Sam Demma, "Be Someone's Taco (Sam Demma)—Breakfast Television," February 24, 2022, YouTube video, https://www.youtube.com/watch?v=pHcqCjj7zYg.

day. Thank me later when this story comes to mind every time you see or eat tacos. You'll never look at them the same way!

MEMENTO MORI

Here's a reminder that might help you live your life to the fullest: one day, you will take your last breath. If you have time to prepare for that moment, the days leading up to it will likely be filled with reflection, and you likely won't be concerned with your accolades and possessions. Those things become meaningless when you leave this planet.

Instead, you'll be thinking about how you treated others, about the impact you made and the legacy you're leaving, and perhaps about what you would have done differently. You might think about how you served others and about how you could have done more to make a positive impact.

Today's society glorifies famous individuals, and there are entire TV channels dedicated to sharing news about them. Yes, they make a huge impact on our world, but it's important we start studying and looking up to servant leaders— people who quietly use their talents to improve the lives of others.

Servant leaders are all around you. When I was growing up, Nonno Sam was my example of this. He always served others before he served himself. I was thirteen years old when he passed away, and I still wish I could have talked to him more about his life and beliefs. Thankfully, my grandmother would share stories with me over the phone whenever I asked. She told me that during the winter, he'd routinely wake up around 4:00 a.m. to shovel the neighbours' driveways before getting ready for work. During the summer, he'd cut the lawns of all the elderly people on his street who couldn't do so for themselves.

One of the people whose grass he cut was 102 years old. When this man found out that Nonno Sam had been diagnosed with cancer, he convinced his son to drive him over to personally thank my grandfather for all the help he'd provided over the years. Another person whose grass he cut had a cat that passed away, and it was Nonno Sam who dug a grave in her backyard to help bury her family member. Talk about being someone's taco. Any time he could use his hands to help, he would.

THERE IS ALWAYS ENOUGH TO GIVE

When they arrived in Canada from Italy, my grandparents had little money. Nonno Sam had to work two jobs. Still, whenever my grandfather was given something, he'd pay it forward.

When he wasn't at the car factory, he worked on a farm. After he'd built trust with the landowner, Nonno Sam was gifted a small plot of land where he could grow his own vegetables. Every season, he'd plant squash and orange zucchini.

When it came time to harvest the crops, my grandfather would pull hundreds of vegetables from the soil and fill his trailer. He'd spend the next few weeks driving to aunts', uncles', and cousins' homes to leave a dozen squash in front of each family member's door. He'd give our family so much that we'd have to give most of it away to our neighbours. They all knew that it had come from Nonno Sam.

His actions taught me that no matter how much or how little you have, there is always enough to give to others. That serving others isn't something you do only after you achieve your version of success—it's a required step on the journey toward your success. Nonno Sam didn't wait until he had enough to give. Instead, he always gave away what he could, and this began his cycle of receiving.

The way my grandfather lived his life taught me that when it comes to serving others, you don't need a degree. To be of service is to make a decision—a decision to help people when you see them in need without any expectation that they'll repay you. This decision isn't always an easy one because it requires you to invest your most important assets: time and energy, and sometimes money.

The irony is that the more time, energy, and money you give to others, the more the world will give you. Receiving anything is often the by-product of giving that same thing away in abundance. Think about it: if you give lots of love, you'll receive an abundance in return; if you spend time serving others, others will want to serve you. Giving, without expectation, is the first step toward receiving.

IT'S NEVER TOO LATE

I'm going to share a vulnerable truth with you: Throughout high school, I was self-absorbed. Don't get me wrong, I was kind to others, but I wouldn't participate in anything that didn't relate to my goal of playing professional soccer. I joined zero clubs and didn't seek out opportunities to serve others or give back until I graduated. It's one of the things I wish I'd done differently.

But it's never too late to change. I recently spoke at a leadership conference, and after the event ended I received the following email from a high school student who'd had a similar experience.

I always knew, from a young age, that I wanted to make a positive change in this world, whether it was big or small. I've been a leader, and I always like to try new things and take on new initiatives. At the beginning of high school, I found myself really wanting to fit in, like most freshmen do.

As a result, I made it my mission to make myself known, and I started joining a bunch of new teams and clubs. I really stepped in with both feet forward. However, I soon began to become centred on popularity, and I associated leadership and making a difference with having a lot of followers and friends.

It took me quite a while to break out of the cycle of craving popularity, and I had to learn the hard way that being a leader isn't associated with being liked by everyone and being popular. In fact, it's quite the opposite. So, I wanted to ask you if you have any advice. How can I really make my difference in this world?

Maybe you're reading this asking yourself the same question. How can you really make your difference in this world?

When I ask myself this question, I'm reminded of how Nonno Sam lived his life. The time he spent going out of his way to help others. The pounds of squash and zucchini he gave away. The snow he shovelled and the grass he cut. I'm also reminded of how Andrew and Emily reacted when they opened the box of tacos. You don't have to change the world to change someone's world. You can make a difference in the world every day! You don't need to wait to be a servant leader, and it's never too late to begin.

Being of service isn't about getting recognition or gaining popularity—it's about putting your head down and doing the work. It's often difficult to be a servant leader, but everyone can do it, including you. The feelings of fulfillment and gratitude you'll get from being of service will overwhelm you. Out of all the small, consistent actions you might take as a result of reading this book, please make sure you include some actions that benefit others.

TAKEAWAYS

- Some of the most meaningful experiences in life come from being of service to others.

- Your small actions have the potential to make a massive impact. You don't have to change the world to change some-one's world.

- Look for opportunities every day to be someone's taco. Strive to use your talents to make a positive difference in the lives of those around you.

- Being of service isn't about getting recognition or popularity—it's about doing the work.

Showing kindness to others is important, and showing kindness to yourself is non-negotiable. Life is challenging enough without constantly worrying whether you're "enough." In the final chapter, we'll discuss the importance of authenticity and avoiding the trap of comparison.

CHAPTER TWELVE

•

CULTIVATE TUNNEL VISION

•

Action: Accept Yourself

By the time I was twenty, comparison was robbing me of my happiness and creativity. Every day, without fail, I experienced feelings of lack and disappointment, and I believed I was moving too slowly. Even on the days when I could honestly say I'd "crushed it," I'd spend twenty to thirty minutes scrolling through social media and focus on all the things I had yet to accomplish.

I'd see inspiring updates from people in my industry, and, although I was happy for them, it consistently made me feel I wasn't doing enough. Can you relate? Maybe when you scroll through your social media feeds you feel the same—you feel behind when you see others seemingly progressing and happy. Deep down, you know something has to change. Remember, things don't change unless you do.

Comparison isn't limited to our online lives, but most of the harmful comparisons I was making were to the social media feeds of people I barely knew.

As I mentioned in Chapter 8, every year on my birthday I give something up. On my twenty-first birthday, it was social media. This meant deleting the apps from both my phone and my computer, and my plan was to stay logged out for an entire year. Many of my peers thought that was extreme and suggested I take a one or two-month break, but I knew I needed a total reset. I needed to develop a tunnel-like focus that eliminated opportunities to feel behind, and I knew giving up social media would help me accomplish this.

If you're anything like I am, you probably spend countless hours staring at your phone each day and then wonder where all your time goes. According to a survey of two thousand people in Britain, the average adult spends the equivalent of thirty-four years of their lives staring at screens—over 4,866 hours a year on average on gadgets such as phones, laptops, and televisions.[39] The number of minutes and seconds is too long to write on these pages.

LOGGING OUT

This study scared me into immediate action. There are so many things I want to do, and the person I want to become can't afford to spend thirty-four years staring at screens. After auditing myself and seeing how much time I spent on social media each day, I decided to log out.

I had three main reasons for making this decision:

- Opportunity cost
- Self-confidence
- Curiosity

---

[39] Emma Elsworthy, "Average Adult Will Spend 34 Years of Their Life Looking at Screens, Poll Claims," *The Independent*, May 11, 2020, https://www.independent.co.uk/life-style/fashion/news/screen-time-average-lifetime-years-phone-laptop-tv-a9508751.html.

Let's look at each one more closely.

Opportunity cost

Every action has a consequence. When you perform a certain action, you cannot be doing something else with that same time and energy. [40] In simple terms, the opportunity cost of an action is everything you sacrifice or turn down when you choose to take that action. If you decide to cut the grass, you can't use that same block of time to go shopping for a new pair of shoes, to cook yourself lunch, or to call your grandmother. The opportunity cost of cutting the grass is missing out on all other alternatives. Start thinking of all your decisions this way and you'll quickly start to discover your priorities. Note: this is not me giving you permission to stop cutting your grass . . .

After auditing my social media usage, I discovered that I was spending about three hours staring at my phone screen each day—and that didn't even include my social media time on my laptop. Three hours each day is 1,095 hours a year, and realizing this raised three questions for me:

What is the opportunity cost of spending all this time on my phone, and am I really learning anything with this large time investment?

Where else could I invest one thousand hours to improve my life?

The potential answers to the above questions were endless, but this process was extremely uncomfortable. It was difficult to face the reality of the situation: I was addicted to social media. Sometimes we'd rather live a lie because we think the pain of change will outweigh the pain of remaining the same.

---

[40] Jason Fernando, "What Is Opportunity Cost?" Investopedia, published March 12, 2022, updated June 27, 2022, https://www.investopedia.com/terms/o/opportunitycost.asp.

But dealing with our uncomfortable truths is what ultimately brings us the most meaning and fulfillment. It's what alleviates our pain. Facing the truth allows us to live a life aligned with our core values. Without the distraction of constant comparison, I knew I could generate more creative ideas and use my time in a more valuable way.

When you make decisions with opportunity cost in mind, you become more comfortable telling people *no*. You make choices based not simply on what someone is offering you, but also on what you could be doing with that time if you decline their offer. You don't have to take this to the extreme with every choice, but, when it comes to big commitments that will require large chunks of time and energy, consider the opportunity cost. No person or activity on this planet is entitled to your time and energy, and you're the gatekeeper to both of those precious resources.

Self-confidence

The second reason for my social media break was related to self-confidence. I knew that every time I went on social media, I experienced a feeling of lack and inferiority. I'd close the apps feeling stressed out and wondering if I was doing enough. If you're on social media right now, it's almost certain that you compare yourself to the content you see and the people you follow, either consciously or subconsciously. The self-talk can quickly become negative: "Look how great their life is"; "You could never do that"; "You're not good-looking"; "You're not doing enough."

If the beliefs you carry in your backpack lead to your future outcomes, speaking negatively to yourself is a recipe for failure.

Comparison can also be the death of excitement—after all, it's hard to recognize your progress and celebrate your journey when you spend all your time glorifying someone else. Often, we know little to nothing about the people we place on pedestals. What someone posts online and what they experience behind the scenes can be worlds apart, so remember that on social media you're comparing your reality to everyone else's perfect highlight reels. Not only that, but the longer you glorify someone else the more assumptions you make about your own self-worth. A quick glance at your social media timeline can result in feelings of doubt, uncertainty, and unworthiness.

To fill the void created by a lack of confidence, you start posting pictures that you think will impress others, and you develop a need to showcase the best aspects of your life. This becomes a loop of validation—a technological drug that grows into an addiction. People begin liking your posts and you experience short-lived happiness and instant gratification, and this reinforcement encourages you to post something similar again, and again. This is the toxic cycle I found myself in. I constantly felt the need to let the entire world know how great I was, while deep down I felt as if I weren't enough.

It's also difficult to be original and authentic when you spend all your time wishing you were like someone else. When I started speaking, I'd constantly compare my ability and progress to those of people who'd been doing it for dozens of years. I tend to speak more out of the left side of my mouth, and I spent weeks trying to "fix" this, thinking people would judge me. The emotions I felt when comparing myself to others and judging my uniqueness led to a lack of passion and creativity.

Success leaves clues, but comparing your first attempt to someone else's one hundredth is a sure way to feel behind.

I thought that taking a break would allow me to detach from this addiction to validation and comparison. The tunnel vision would give me peace of mind and the space to define success for myself.

When the need to feel significant and successful begins to negatively affect your mental health, explore why. There's nothing wrong with sharing your achievements online, but never forget that most people aren't sharing their failures or struggles. Social media is mostly a one-sided conversation without the full context and perspective.

Curiosity

The third reason I took a year off social media was to conduct a curious experiment. I had my twenty-first birthday in the middle of the COVID-19 pandemic, when social media usage was at an all-time high because people were stuck at home with nothing else to do. I wondered what would happen if I did the exact opposite from everyone else for an entire year.

Some of my best ideas have come from asking, "What if?" During an interview with Jay Shetty, rapper Russ shared the best advice he'd ever received: "What if it could turn out better than you ever imagined?"[41] "What if" is such a powerful statement because it opens your mind and imagination to endless possibilities.

UNEXPECTED BONUSES

These were the three reasons behind my decision, but as the experiment unfolded I uncovered more benefits than I'd expected. I not only increased

---

[41] Jay Shetty Podcast, "Russ ON: Delusional Self-Confidence & How to Start Manifesting Your Dream Life," May 3, 2021, YouTube video, 57:48, https://www.youtube.com/watch?v=-4c61A2VD8k.

my self-confidence, I also boosted my creativity, got back into the best physical shape of my life, and experienced more business growth than ever.

Despite the popular belief that people would forget about me and my speaking career would be destroyed, the opposite happened. The grass isn't greener on the other side—it's greener where you water it. Instead of constantly comparing myself to others, I was working to create the life that I wanted to live. I devoted the time I would have spent scrolling through other people's lives to actions that helped me bring my dreams closer to reality: making sales calls, journaling, reading, and getting more sleep. Over time, I stopped feeling the need to show everyone how great I was. What began to matter most was how I saw myself.

For the record, I didn't last the entire year, but for a good reason. I returned to social media after eight months to release a graduation video for the class of 2021. It was a creative project that I worked on during my social media detox, and it made sense to release it before the school year ended. That project reached more than one hundred thousand students, was featured on four national news stations, and was screened in schools across North America.[42] I'm confident that it wouldn't have come to life as quickly as it did if I'd been spending four hours a day on my phone.

Do you need to take a break from social media? That's not something I can decide for you, but I will tell you this: if you feel as if you're not doing enough, moving too slowly, or not as successful as you "need to be," and these feelings are negatively affecting your mental health, it's something you should seriously consider.

---

[42] Sam Demma, "Dear Class of 2021 (Your Story Isn't over) I Sam Demma," May 13, 2021, YouTube video, 4:48, https://www.youtube.com/watch?v=JB-pzvaFQTU.

CONGRATULATIONS, YOU'RE HUMAN!

You don't have to be on social media to compare yourself to others, and it takes only seconds to make a mental comparison. Growing up, while walking down the halls of my school I'd glance at other students' shoes, watches, and expensive clothes, and I would immediately remind myself of the things I didn't have. And I had more than enough—the comparison just seemed to happen naturally. On the soccer field, I'd compare my skills to those of my teammates and the opposing players. By the poolside or on the beach, I'd compare my physique to the other men with their shirts off.

I'd walk past people who had clear, smooth skin and my mind would remind me that I had a full face of acne. For two years, I'd routinely break out in dozens of pimples on my face, back, and chest. My mom took me to see dermatologists, skin care specialists, and anyone she thought might be able to help; meanwhile, my embarrassment stopped me from taking part in social activities. I used makeup to cover the blemishes for picture day in school, and my bathroom was filled with products that burned my skin. Looking back, I can see that I struggled so much during that phase not because of my acne but because of society's beauty standards. The models and celebrities everyone idolized all seemed to have the perfect facial and physical features, and at the time I didn't realize that there were teams of people dedicated to making these individuals "perfect"—as if that's a real thing.

Whatever "flaw" you think you have, understand that you're not alone—everyone you know has insecurities. When you discover yours, laugh and remember these words: "Congratulations, you're human!"

Life is too short to worry about a red bump on your face or to stress over the things you don't have, and comparing yourself to others won't change a thing. Instead, strive to accept every aspect of who you are, and if that means challenging beauty standards, changing who you follow online, and removing yourself from situations that make you feel inferior, do it!

Many of the comparisons we make hinge on other people's beliefs. Empty those beliefs from your backpack and embrace the journey that is your life. Find the spaces where you can be your authentic self.

TRIED AND TESTED

The concept of removing yourself from others' influence and cultivating tunnel vision isn't a new one. In the Christian faith, there's a parable where Jesus retreats to the desert alone for forty days to fast and discern his future plans.

Jay Shetty, the influential speaker, author, and podcast host, is best known for his videos about spending three years living as a monk to find himself, his values, and his calling. Many artists will "disappear" for years to work on their next album or creative project—Kendrick Lamar is just one example.

Tunnel vision has benefited many great visionaries. It helped me break free of my addiction to social media, build a sense of self-confidence detached from the validation of others, significantly grow my speaking business, and find more time every day to be present and enjoy the journey of life.

TAKEAWAYS

- Every decision you make has an opportunity cost. Choose where you invest your time and energy wisely.

- Tunnel vision helps you realize that the grass isn't greener on the other side: it's greener where you water it.

- Success leaves clues, but comparing your first attempt to someone else's one hundredth is a sure way to feel behind.

- There's nothing wrong with admiring others' achievements, but never forget that most people aren't sharing their failures or struggles.

- Everyone you know has insecurities; when you discover yours, congratulate yourself on being human!

When you stop comparing yourself to others, you'll increase your confidence, encourage your creativity, and feel inspired to fearlessly pursue your boldest ambitions. As extreme as it might sound, this might require time away from social media and situations where you feel inferior. When you stop checking how green everyone else's grass looks, you can take care of your own. Stop the comparison and start living your authentic life.

CONCLUSION

If you haven't already, crack a smile and give yourself a pat on the back. You just finished a book! Seriously, though, you've invested time in yourself, and that's worth celebrating. Treat yourself to something you love as a reward for your dedication to learning and personal development.

You've exposed your mind to beliefs and actions that have the power to enhance your life. Reading drastically changed my mindset and helped me start thinking bigger, and I hope this book has done the same for you.

With new beliefs in your backpack, approach your days with the intention of bringing your ideas to life through small, consistent actions. You'll move closer to your dreams and start creating a life of meaning.

The beliefs and actions you've discovered within these pages have the power to alter your future—but only if you choose to do something with them. Knowledge is only as powerful as your willingness to act on it. Decide, right now, that you're going to do something with the information you just learned.

To help you get the most out of this book, choose a chapter, reread it, and figure out how you're going to implement its learnings. Repeat this process for the next twelve months, dedicating one month to each chapter. Not sure where to start? The following pages give you a recap of everything you just learned.

Empty Your Backpack

Belief: You Define You

You carry an invisible backpack on your shoulders. Over time, this bag fills up with your own experiences as well as the beliefs that other people place on you. If you don't stop to look inside this bag and remove the beliefs of others, you can end up living a life that's not yours, making decisions based on others' beliefs rather than your own desires.

After removing the limiting ideas that other people place on you, repack your bag with people who believe in you and the beliefs of people doing exactly what you want to do. Success leaves clues, so find role models and soak up their mentalities.

Adjust Your Timeline

Belief: There Is No Right Path or Time

Society does a great job of painting a picture of the perfect life timeline. If yours looks different, you naturally feel resistance. What society rarely tells you is that every path is valid and every person is different. It's time to stop living your life based on what everyone else is doing. Instead, create your own path and live life on your timeline.

Others may get upset if your life choices challenge their beliefs, but any disappointment they may have is nothing compared to the regret you might feel if you live in a way that isn't aligned with your heart and intuition.

Be Persistent

Belief: Rejection Is an Opportunity

You've heard the word *no* thousands of times, and, whether you realize it or not, it's likely been a barrier to your progress. It's time to redefine this word.

Every time you hear the word *no* **in a business and personal-growth context**, instead of interpreting it as *stop*, ask yourself, "How can I show this person how much I care about the opportunity? How can I get creative in my approach?" When you start reframing a business-related *no* in your mind and face your fear of rejection, there's nothing to stop you from achieving your goals and dreams.

Build Your Tower of Trash

Belief: You Decide What's Possible

Your beliefs lead to your success. If you believe something is impossible before you try, you've already set yourself up for failure. On the other hand, if you believe that what you want is possible, you're already halfway there. The things you accomplish depend on the beliefs that you carry.

Change your beliefs and everything else will change. Your beliefs lead to how you feel, your feelings lead to the actions you take, and your actions lead to your results; so, if you're not getting the results you'd like, it's not enough to change your actions. You need to address the root of the problem—what you're choosing to believe. You don't need special skills, unique connections, or superior knowledge to bring your ideas to life. Your ability to achieve your dreams rests on your personal beliefs—everything else is secondary.

Dream Big

Belief: There Are No Limits

As you grow up, you set aside fewer and fewer moments to dream. You dampen your imagination because you're taught it gets you nowhere in the "real world." Rather than pursuing who you want to become, you settle for what will "get you by."

Never stop dreaming. Understanding who you want to become will help you determine your path, and dreaming keeps you excited for the future and energized to tackle whatever obstacles stand in your way. Your dreams don't have to be huge, but they need to be yours.

Connect the Dots

Belief: Trust Your Intuition

Steve Jobs believed that you can't make sense of certain events in your life until they become a piece of your past—that only in hindsight can you understand why things unfolded as they did. I can confidently tell you that all the difficult decisions I've made led me to become who I am today. In hindsight, they all make sense.

Following your heart can be difficult when you're unsure if your efforts are going to pay off. As hard as it may seem, have faith in your decisions. Trust that at some point in your future the dots will connect. Living your life with this mindset will ensure you stay true to your values, despite the difficult choices you'll be forced to make.

Commit to Small, Consistent Actions

Action: Be Consistent

Change takes time. Most people don't achieve their dreams because they lack the patience required to allow time to compound their efforts. Our society has advanced to the point where you can want something today and get it tomorrow; this is great for everyday needs but terrible for your dreams. We've been conditioned to believe that the effort and time required between wanting and receiving is minimal. Instead of falling prey to this desire for instant gratification, remind yourself that change takes time and the only sure way to bring your dreams to life is through many small, consistent actions.

The step that stops most people is the first one. *Small, consistent actions* is a reminder that all you need to focus on is the next step. Over time, with patience and consistency, those small steps result in massive change. Stop convincing yourself that your idea is too big. Stop convincing yourself that the project will require too much work. Instead, figure out the next smallest action. Once you complete it, move on to the next one.

Remove the Cookies from the Pantry

Action: Make the Sacrifice

We all have vices, those things we enjoy but that hold us back from growth in some way. When I was growing up, I'd go to my nonna's house and she'd tell me I was too thin; but in the doctor's office, I was told the exact opposite. I still remember the day my doctor told me I had to stop eating so many sausages, olives, and cheese or I'd become obese. To make progress and bring your dreams to life, remove anything from your environment that may tempt you into an action that won't help you.

Resisting temptation is easy when you have no other option. Don't give yourself one.

Act on Your Ideas

Action: Get Creative

Your imagination and your creative ideas are two of your greatest assets. There's a reason that ideas are called "intellectual property"—they hold serious value. And it's a myth that creativity is something people are born with. It's a result of discipline. Decide to set aside distraction-free time with a blank sheet of paper and a pen to think about creative solutions to a problem, and you will generate unique ideas.

Use your creative ideas to bring your dreams to life. Use them to stand out. Look at what everyone else is doing and come up with a creative way to do the opposite.

Make Something from Nothing

Action: Tap into Your Resourcefulness

Your success doesn't depend on what you have or how talented you are. Your resourcefulness—your willingness to do whatever it takes—is what determines your success.

Keep in mind that *resourceful* does not mean *impatient*. The timing of your success is not within your control. A dream might require an investment of two days, two weeks, or ten years, so you must develop the patience to embrace the time necessary to bring your dream to life, trusting that things will work out in your future.

Be Someone's Taco

Action: Serve Others

Serving others isn't something you do only after you achieve your version of success—it's part of the journey to your success. When you serve others, you feel good, the person you help benefits, and the world as a whole becomes a slightly better place. It was my grandfather who taught me, through his actions, that life is the most meaningful when we serve others.

Being a servant leader isn't about getting recognition or gaining popularity. It's about putting your head down and doing the work. It can be difficult, but everyone can do it. Don't wait to get involved—add acts of service to your to-do list to start creating a more meaningful life right now.

Cultivate Tunnel Vision

Action: Accept Yourself

It's hard to feel like you're making progress toward your dreams when every time you go online you're bombarded by the seemingly perfect lives of everyone else. Consistently focusing on others' lives can generate feelings of lack, and the comparison game you begin playing—your own reality versus what people post online—can be a slippery slope to a total loss of confidence.

Some of the most influential and inspiring leaders realized that to do great work, they needed tunnel vision. They needed time to focus on their work without noise from the outside world. If you want success, there will be moments on your journey when you'll require tunnel vision. When you stop the comparisons, you'll increase your confidence, encourage your creativity, and fearlessly pursue your boldest ambitions.

THE BEGINNING

The rest of your life starts right now—make the most of it. No one can do the work for you, and I promise you that no one will care about your dreams as much as you do. Others may try to tell you what you should do, but you have to decide for yourself what kind of life you want to create and live.

My hope is that this book provided you with insights and examples that will help you feel more courageous and confident in your ability to create your remarkable life. Chasing your dreams and finding meaning starts with a decision to do so, and taking the time to read this book means you've already begun. Keep moving in this direction—you're on a good path. (Remember, there is no "right" path.)

One final note: Life is filled with thousands of games, and it's okay to change the game you're playing. It's okay to change your dream, just don't stop dreaming!

GET IN TOUCH

The thing about writing a book is that you never know who will read it and enjoy it. You and I may never meet—and I'm kinda not okay with that! So, I created an email address and PO box dedicated to conversations between my readers and me.

You can email me or send me a letter anytime. Your thoughts on the book, your general feedback, or your stories about changing your beliefs, chasing your dreams, and creating a life of meaning would make my day. I look forward to hearing from you.

Email address:
book@samdemma.com

PO Box:
1822 Whites Road, N. Suite #208
Pickering, Ontario, Canada
L1V 0B1

RESOURCES

Influential books:

- Brown, Brené. *Dare to Lead*. New York: Random House, 2018.

- Carnegie, Dale. *How to Win Friends and Influence People*. New York: Simon and Schuster, 1936.

- Cialdini, Robert. *Influence, New and Expanded: The Psychology of Persuasion*. New York: Harper Business, 2021.

- Coelho, Paulo. *The Alchemist*. Translated by Alan R. Clarke. New York: HarperOne, 1993.

- Covey, Stephen. *The 7 Habits of Highly Effective People*. Provo, UT: Covey Leadership Center, 1996.

- Deida, David. *The Way of the Superior Man*. Boulder, CO: Sounds True, 2017.

- Dweck, Carol. *Mindset*. New York: Ballantine Books, 2006.

- Haley, Alex, and Malcolm X. *The Autobiography of Malcolm X*. New York: Ballantine Books, 1965.

- Hill, Napoleon. *Think and Grow Rich*. Meriden, CT: The Ralston Society, 1937.

- Jackson, Curtis. *Hustle Harder, Hustle Smarter*. New York: Amistad, 2020.

- Kenner, Rob. *The Marathon Don't Stop: The Life and Times of Nipsey Hussle*. New York: ATRIA, 2022.

- Kim, W. Chan and Renée Mauborgne. *Blue Ocean Strategy*. Boston, MA: Harvard Business Review Press, 2015.

- Robbins, Tony. *Awaken the Giant Within*. New York: Simon and Schuster, 1992.

- Rohn, Jim. *The Seasons of Life*. Jim Rohn International, 1981.

- Ruiz, don Miguel. *The Four Agreements*. San Rafael, CA: Amber-Allen Publishing, Inc., 1997.

- Russ. *It's All in Your Head*. New York: Harper Design, 2019.

Inspiring podcasts:

- Idea Generation, with Noah Callahan-Bever,
  https://www.ideageneration.com/content.

- On Purpose, with Jay Shetty, https://jayshetty.me/podcast/.

- The Goal Digger Podcast, with Jenna Kutcher,
  https://jennakutcherblog.com/goal-digger-podcast/.

- The Growth League, with Diana Kander,
  https://dianakander.com/podcast/.

- The High Performing Student, with Sam Demma,
  https://samdemma.com/high-performing-student-podcast/.

- The Joe Rogan Experience, with Joe Rogan,
  https://www.joerogan.com/#jre-section.

- The Sports Motivation Podcast, with Niyi Sobo,
  https://imnotyou.com/smp/.

- The Tim Ferris Show, with Tim Ferris, https://tim.blog/podcast/.

- The Tony Robbins Podcast, with Tony Robbins,
  https://www.tonyrobbins.com/podcasts/.

Want more resources?
Email book@samdemma.com

ABOUT THE AUTHOR

SAM DEMMA is the youngest board director of the Canadian Association of Professional Speakers. A highly requested keynote speaker in the education space, Demma has delivered over three hundred presentations for clients who want to create a culture of hope, service, and self-belief. He is routinely invited for interviews on national media outlets and has been featured on the TEDx platform twice.

As a high school student, he co-founded PickWaste, a grassroots initiative that mobilized youth to pick up garbage in their communities. Within five years, the organization filled more than three thousand bags of trash and provided students with six thousand meaningful volunteer hours. The success of the initiative confirmed for Demma how small, consistent actions can have a significant impact, and he lives that message in all he does.

Following his keynote presentations, students and educators often commit to performing more acts of kindness, taking small, consistent actions toward their personal goals, and proactively looking for ways to be of service to others. In his spare time, Demma dances the bachata, eats handfuls of tacos, and works to convince people that pineapples do not belong on pizza. For more information and booking inquiries please visit: **www.samdemma.com**.